WHY THE FUCK AM I STILL DRINKING

A no-bullshit guide to breaking the patterns that keep you stuck

Why the Fuck Am I Still Drinking:
A no-bullshit guide to breaking the patterns that keep you stuck

Te' Youngblood
Published by: Desirable Phoenix LLC
Cover Design by Te' Youngblood

Published in the United States of America

Contents

My Journey:
A Year of Growth & Transformation

This section highlights significant points in the start of my no drinking journey. For a year, I kept journals of everything that happened in my life from the emotions that I had to the days when I felt lost. This will give you an idea of what it looks like to heal while giving you a true glimpse of the changes that were made and how they affected my life month by month.

These changes are not indicative of the only changes you can make; it is only a guide. Your changes and results will vary. I could not foresee the changes I made in the following months, and every step was a revolutionary turning point in my life.

January 2023

This is the month that it started all. On January 1, 2023, I had my last bottle of wine with a friend. On January 2, 2023, I went cold turkey. I bought a brand-new journal and kept a record of my day-to-day thoughts and emotions, and I wrote almost every day.

My focus word for 2023 was consistency because I wanted to become more consistent in my life and in my business. I decided that the habits I would be consistent with were waking up at 6am, posting every day on Tik Tok to grow my following and do the no alcohol challenge for 90-days.

Over the course of the month, I saw minuscule improvements in my mood. Getting up early helped me have more time for myself before I went to work, and I didn't have to rush off to get there on time. I could do my Tik Toks, eat breakfast, and read all before work. I felt like I was able to focus on my business and myself first, then at the end of the day I wasn't dragging myself to do business tasks because I had gotten them done beforehand.

My mood around work started to fade from anger to indifference. Situations that would normally bother me no longer affected me. I decided that I was going to show up differently in my relationships and friendships. I wanted to be more attentive and really be intentional with how I interacted with the people in my life.

In this month, there were many times that I wanted to drink. I wanted to drink after the first day of not drinking, but I kept my head. It was difficult, especially when I started to have big emotions, and I held it together.

February 2023

I started to notice mental changes from not drinking. I could tell that I was becoming more aware of my friends and what was going on in their lives. I began to show up and at the same time, I was able to see where my relationships with others were. My mood and clarity improved.

Over the month, I had a lot of emotions come up and I could see that things in my life were shifting. I didn't know what changes would happen, but I knew they were coming.

March 2023

My two best friends and I planned a trip for the beginning of March to Las Vegas. I got a lot of comments about how people would have to start drinking just to go to Vegas and saying how strong I was for not drinking there. There had been a lot that I wanted to do with my time in Vegas, and that was spend time with my friends, get away from my life at home, and reevaluate my life.

You know how they say that things get worse before they get better? Well, this is where I saw that saying come to life. Leading up to, during and after my trip, my world started to fall apart.

During the time I was there, I could see the issues in my relationships more clearly. There were things that I had done and not done, and also things that had been done or not done on my partner's part. Although I saw where I was lacking and started to make changes and showed up differently, the damage had already been done.

Two weeks after I came home from Vegas, I started my 8-week chakra alignment and broke up with one of my partners. My emotional health declined significantly after this breakup. I cannot remember a time when I felt this low.

This chakra alignment was different this time. It was like the fog over my life had been lifted and every meditation that I did brought me closer to my needs, my wants, my desires. It was the catalyst for all the steps I took on my journey. My 90-day challenge was closing in, and I decided to keep it going until the end of the alignment.

April 2023

As my emotional health declined, I searched for new ways to help relieve emotions and feel better. No matter what I did, I could not figure out what was wrong. It felt like my emotions shut down, and it physically hurt to feel. I didn't want to feel emotions anymore and I put my walls up to shut people out.

I discovered ways to energetically heal and process what was going on emotionally. In the month of April, I continued to feel like I had no emotions, but it would take some time before I felt like myself again.

During this month, a friend of mine came to see me after she found out about my breakup. Even though I did not want to give my energy to anyone, this visit lit a different fire in me. The energy exchange between us was all love and nurture. The words she spoke to me were genuine, healing, and lit a fire of change in me.

My attitude about work and my coworkers had gotten better, but I knew that I did not want to be there any longer. After this visit, I decided to put my resume up on Indeed and an employer reached out to me within a couple of days. They reached out to me on April 6th, and I had a job by April 19th. I put in my two weeks at my old job and the rest is history.

May 2023

April and May were months of energetic healing. I explored Accunect, Body Code, and continued my NET sessions. In each of these sessions I discovered that the emotion I had been feeling since the breakup was despair. During these sessions, I energetically released the emotions of sadness and processed the baggage that came along with the relationships I lost.

Before starting my new job, I took a week off to finish processing the breakup and to get myself back on track. The new work environment was better. The beginning days were chaotic since they had been without a person in my position for about two months. I was a lot happier and could feel my emotions starting to come back online.

Around this time, I needed help to release and manage stress, so I started running. As for my relationships, I continued to watch the people in my circle and weed them out. My walls started to fall, but I was still very cautious with my emotions.

The 8-week chakra alignment ended, and I decided that I would go the rest of the year and not drink alcohol.

June 2023

At this point in the year, I was still not drinking but I stopped getting up early.

I contracted out to my old job until the new person was trained and able to maintain the position I had once held. It was nice working for the extra money. This is when I learned about giving to myself more. I had never been a person to buy myself things, but this was something I started to do to show myself appreciation. I bought new shoes, clothes, and even ice cream, just because. I allowed myself to buy something for me because I wanted to. I wanted to show myself that I could also treat myself because I worked for it.

This one action made me realize that I can take care of bills and my responsibilities and still treat myself. I am worth it.

I noticed that my boundaries grew stronger. Before I stopped drinking, I would let people cross my boundaries. I knew that I was not enforcing them. I wanted to keep people in my life, and I knew that in order to feel comfortable in my skin again, I had to say something. I realized I love myself more than I knew and would rather deal with people who respect my boundaries than someone who doesn't respect them.

July 2023

This month, I started to get up at 6:00 am again, and although my chakra alignment had ended, I started to meditate daily.

I started to see opportunities everywhere in my life, and I took full advantage of them.

At some point, I began an outline to a book that I thought I was going to write, but I didn't take it that far.

I started to understand my limits and my boundaries, and what I needed to do to protect myself and my peace. I became more confident in my decisions, and I picked up a new hobby, gardening.

August 2023

This month was a bit of an adventure for me.

I could feel a shift in my career goals. It felt like I was out of alignment with my mission. At the time, I was not sure what it could be, and I brainstormed with my best friend to figure out what I wanted to do. I wanted to help people, but I felt like I was sitting on the sidelines creating rather than actually helping them.

As the business ideas were swirling in my head, so were many other thoughts about my life and how I had gotten here. After thinking about my life, relationships, and the people who I left behind, I wrote a 40-page letter in my journal. It was everything that I had wanted to say to one specific person, and after I wrote it, I felt 100% better. The only thing that saddened me was that this person would never read it, and even if they did, they would never understand it.

This was also the month that I was given an alcoholic beverage at a restaurant when I asked for a non-alcoholic drink. This incident made me realize how important my goal of not drinking was to me. I had a lot of support and friends who reassured me that I was not to blame for this snafu. I was devastated. I sulked for about 12 hours and after that period was over, I felt better about what had happened.

September 2023

After the brainstorming session with my best friend on my career goals and what I wanted to do business wise, I started the process of writing the book you have in your hands. Over Labor Day weekend, I camped out in my backyard, and I worked. I outlined my first draft which was the easiest thing I had written. I meditated outside in nature, and I painted. I read books and I nurtured my soul.

Later in the month, I went to Florida to visit one of my best friends and had a beautiful time in the sun. It was a much-needed trip.

This was the month that I decided to declutter my home, and work on my financial situation.

<u>**October 2023**</u>

This was the month of rest. I could feel that I needed to take a break, or else burnout would find me. During this time, I decluttered my house more which helped me feel lighter and think clearly. It made me feel like I was getting rid of the things that kept me tied to my thoughts and emotions that I no longer needed. I realized that this space that I was living in was mine to do what I wanted, and I started to decorate my house the way that I wanted to.

I could feel that I was getting anxious and impatient. I was anticipating changes in my life, and although I did not know what they were, I wanted them to come quickly. I made a lot of moves this month that I should have waited on. I lost friends, and potential relationships because I wanted to move faster.

<u>**November 2023**</u>

Over this month, I decided that I needed to recalibrate my heart, mind, and purpose.

My book was coming along great, and my life was aligning. I no longer felt like I was "forcing" relationships with others, and I was happy to be free of stress and worrying.

For Thanksgiving, I decided to drive to Georgia to visit my best friend and spend Thanksgiving with her and her family. It was during this time that I realized how important family was to me and what I needed to do to spend more time with them.

<u>**December 2023**</u>

In the last month of the year, I felt accomplished. I made it to the end of the year with no alcohol which was a huge accomplishment for me. My boyfriend and I went to see a Pittsburgh Steelers game in Pennsylvania and had a great anniversary weekend.

I started to see that my time was more valuable than I had been treating it. I was no longer going to let others dictate the time that I have on this Earth. I would move forward in my life and make the decisions that felt right for me. Nothing was holding me back and I had to break through the barriers I set up for myself.

I was paying attention to what my body needed mentally, physically and emotionally, and I was making better choices overall. I started closing energy leaks that I held onto or hadn't dealt with in my home and relationships, and I saw that my life had changed in so many ways.

Introduction

In 2022, a study by the Fisher College of Business wrote an article that said in America, 9% of people complete their New Years' resolutions, 23% of people quit their resolution by the end of week one, and 43% of people quit by the end of January. It is hard from these statistics to say how many people actually try to quit drinking a year either as a New Years' Resolution or a challenge for themselves.

However, The Recovery Village website states that over 30% of people who attempt to stop drinking will relapse in the first year of sobriety, and that rate goes down over time. https://www.therecoveryvillage.com/alcohol-abuse/alcohol-relapse-statistics/. There are trends like Dry January and Sober October, that get thrown into the mix, so it is hard to tell the actual number of people who attempt to stop drinking every year.

When a person decides that they are going to stop drinking, the why differs amongst them. When it comes to the trend months to stop drinking, the idea is to detox their bodies from alcohol because they feel they have overconsumed, or they want to give their bodies a break. I knew a woman who decided to stop drinking for two weeks because she was told that she may have gout and that not drinking would help the symptoms. The trend does not usually lead to long-term quitting, but it may help some decide to slow down their drinking or even quitting for good.

My name is Te' and I am a mind, body, and soul coach. I started out my journey knowing that I wanted to help others heal from trauma and over time it became more.

My journey began with reconnecting to my body. I did not realize how disconnected I felt from my body until I decided to try yoga. I started with yoga, which helped with being mindful and loosened the hold that I had to control everything in my life. It is a practice that helps you to be present in your body and connect on a deeper level, and that is exactly what I needed. Years later, I decided to try pole fitness, not only to connect more with my physical body, but also to connect more with my sensual side and movement. The exploration of pole fitness, movement, and my ideals on sexiness started to play a major role in my healing journey, and I became a pole fitness instructor to help others connect with their bodies physically, sensually, and intimately. It also helped that I was a sexual health educator and helped women explore their sexuality, desires in the bedroom, what it meant to be sexy, and how to empower them to ask for what they want not only in the bedroom, but also in life.

As I learned about different modalities of healing, it eventually led me to learn more about energy healing and chakra alignments. As I explored going to energy healers, I decided that I could use this method to help others as well. I became a Practical Reiki Master so that I could use it as a tool to help others shift the energy in themselves and to help them heal. This is part of spiritual coaching that helps nourish the soul.

As I continued the route of teaching others to overcome their past, I came across a certification program to learn Mental Health First Aid. Mental Health First Aid is an evidence-based, early-intervention course that teaches participants about mental health and substance use challenges, which is exactly what I needed to help the very people I was coaching.

Over the last nine years, I have dedicated myself to learning the ends and outs of trauma, energy, change, and transformation. I have lived through a lifetime of challenges and fought through obstacles to get where I am. My dream has always been to help those who have been through what I have overcome and push forward in their lives. I have helped over 200 people do just that.

The book that you are reading now was an accident. I did not intend to write a book about my no alcohol journey, but after I stopped drinking for nine months, the book literally fell out of me. I had a conversation with my best friend about not feeling aligned in my business and I really just wanted to sell my first book. We talked about how much had changed since I stopped drinking and my friend said, "I think that means you need to write another book." And that was that. On Labor Day Weekend of 2023, I started the outline and draft of this book.

I have always read books on how to better yourself, influence others, how to be a badass, or even how to make a decision and move in a short amount of time. One of the biggest differences in this book is that it gives you steps on how to look inside yourself for the answers you seek. You peel apart the onion of your emotions, analyze what you are avoiding and acknowledge the changes you need to make to take that leap of faith and change them.

This book is for the person who feels lost within themselves. The one who has never truly "dated" themselves or given themselves the time of day. The one who doesn't know what their own peace looks like or how to find it, what they like to do, who they are or how to find themselves. The one struggling to set boundaries or enforce the ones they have set. The one whose coping mechanisms aren't working anymore – who feels triggered, drained, and stuck, but doesn't know how to break free.

This book is for you if you are:
- Tired of complaining about your life but unsure how to change it;
- Avoiding change because it feels scary, overwhelming, or pointless;
- Someone who believe you have to start completely over to heal – and feels paralyzed by that idea;
- A businesswoman burned out from the corporate grind, ready for something different;
- A man at his wits' end, questioning whether there's any fight left in him;
- Someone who has been trying (and failing) to stop a bad habit for years – and you're finally ready to figure out why; and,
- An endless to-do list maker and never seems to get anything done.

This book isn't about sugarcoating the process of change and transformation. It's about meeting yourself exactly where you are – raw, real, and ready for change – and learning how to actually move forward. If you're fed up with your own pattens but still holding on to a flicker of hope that life can feel different – this book is for you.

It is the guide to finding yourself so that you can be the person you have always dreamed of. The person that stays sheltered because you believe that no one will like them, or accept them, and that they will be criticized for living their life the way they want to. That person deserves a chance to live. That person deserves a voice. And every time I sat down at my computer, that is who I was writing for. So that one day, every person who reads this finds their true path and begins to walk it, happier, healthier, and full of excitement to take the next step.

For the last nine years, I had it in my mind that I was going to help people overcome trauma. The reality is that I had suffered and knew that others were suffering too, and I got tired of it. I was tired of being in the exact same place, making the exact same choices and getting nowhere. I wanted a new life. I wanted to be happier. I wanted to be better. I wanted to get the fuck out of survival mode because that is where I had been since my ex-husband left in 2019. I felt so helpless like there was no one there to help me through my traumatic experience. I was reliving the shame, pain, and guilt every day, at every job, every time I drank, and every failed relationship. I began writing the book that I was looking for in that bookstore when I felt lost and confused about what I was going to do. The guide that would help me change inside and out so that I could find happiness, joy, and excitement in my life. The book that would help me see how I made the decision to be in the mess I made, and how to finally remove it from my life. I wrote this book because it did not exist in the time when I needed it most.

Here's the thing, I've read a lot of self-help books. Some are straightforward, some are cute, and some have no fluff, but too many still dance around the real shit. You're going to spend your time wherever you choose to whether that's reading this book or putting it down for another. But if you stay, this book will guide you through a soul-deep transformation: calling out your own bullshit, breaking free from the pain you keep running back to, and helping you rebuild a life rooted in real self-trust and unapologetic identity. I don't just talk about healing. I lived the cycle, broke it, and built the blueprint. This is the raw, uncomfortable, liberating truth your soul's been craving. No fluff. No sugarcoating. No apologies.

Woody Allen said, "if you want to hear God laugh, tell him about your plans." In this book, you are going to find many ways to change your habits and create a better life for yourself. Not only will you learn the exact methods I used to stop drinking, and create healthier habits, you will learn what you are thinking, how you are feeling, and what your body needs to fulfill the dream you have for your life. But this isn't a book you just read… It's a book you *experience*. Each chapter will challenge you with exercises that pull your truth to the surface. You'll uncover the habits, beliefs, and emotional patterns holding you back and you'll build new ones that push you forward.

This is hands-on healing. Every chapter, every exercise, every uncomfortable moment you lean into will be a building block to the life you actually want to live.

We will talk about how to navigate the feelings, emotions and earth-shattering situations that will happen as you go through your journey. You will read stories about people's lives and see how these methods can be used practically in your everyday life. At the end of each chapter, we will celebrate your success, and we will create those celebrations together.

My promise to you is that once you have done the activities and exercises in this book, you will be the author of your life again in a few short months. You will be more confident in your decisions, and you will be happier than when you started.

A word of caution: You will not see changes overnight. You have been following the same path and repeating the same patterns for years. You have gotten yourself into a mess and it is going to take cleaning up that mess to set things right again. If you believe that one chapter, one activity, or one journal entry is going to change your life instantly, this book is not for you. The only way this book will not work is if you don't.

It took me 14 months of consistent work to put out a fourth draft of this book, and more months in editing to make sure that this book was as perfect as I could get it. When I wrote my first book, *Tainted: Overcoming the Stigma of Sexual Trauma*, it took me a total of six years to write and publish it. That does not include all of my high school, and college years talking about how I was going to write a book. That subject matter was a bit heavier and each time I picked it up, I saw the book in a different way. It never got easier to write it. So by the time I wanted to edit it and change the way it was formatted, I was tired of looking at it. Literally! It got to a point where I would sit down to edit and I would think to myself, well… I could be doing something else. Or I don't think that changing anything is going to make my first book any better, but I also wanted it to be the perfect self-help book.

I talked to my best friend and other friends who knew I was writing a book, and they were like, "Will you just publish it already? Done is done. It is complete enough. And besides, you can release a second edition later." So, I just published it.

This book that you are holding in your hands, reading on your tablet, or listening to has been a labor of love. I was surprised how easily the book came to me from outline to my final draft. *Why The Fuck Am I Still Drinking* homes in on a piece of my healing journey and shows you the exact steps to make a change in your life in as little as three months. Make a commitment to yourself and follow through. Get up early. Start your workout. Eat healthier. Quit smoking. Whatever your goal is, start now. Take one step each day towards your overall goal and watch how your life and everything in it begins to shift. No more sulking around, doing nothing and then bitching about how things aren't any different. Got it?

Here is my warning…

There were a lot of things that I was not prepared for when I decided to quit drinking. We as coaches, teachers and consultants glorify the "end" of the journey. We discuss and exalt how amazing we feel and how happy we are and how grateful we are for the things we have accomplished. It is rare that we talk about the parts that no one sees. If we do talk about them, the majority of us talk about it very briefly. So I am going to start off this book with the top five things that I learned, and throughout this book I will go over them in greater detail.

1.   This journey is lonely as hell, but it's not long-term.

No one could have prepared me for the deep loneliness that I would feel throughout this process. When I started the no alcohol challenge, I had two friends who decided to take part in it with me. The difference: we were not doing the challenge for the same reasons. I knew that my reasons went deeper than just detoxing for three months, and as time went on and I began to see the changes take place, I realized that I did not have people in my camp who felt the same way or used alcohol in the same way.

There were people in my life who criticized me for not drinking when I went to Las Vegas with my girls, and even one person who asked if they thought I was able to not drink when I went to a bar. My circle got smaller. I realized that drinking was one of the things that I had in common with most of my friends and when I stopped, I decided that those were not the people I wanted to be around.

I implore you that if and when it happens, continue to push through. On the other side of this loneliness is finding yourself and finding the people who fit the person you have wanted to become.

2.   Your patterns got you here and you will stay here until you change them.

The definition of insanity is doing the same thing over and over again and expecting a different result. Most people do not want to come to terms with the fact that they have put themselves in the situation that they are in.

This could be due to a number of things that have happened in their life, and the reality is they have the power to change it. The problem is that the methods they have used in the past are patterns that never fell away.

Think of it this way: You decide that you want to make store bought cookies. You take the cookies out of the package, put them on the baking sheet and place them in the over. After 15 minutes you check them, and the cookies are not baking. You look at the package of cookies, you take more out, you put them on the sheet, and place more in the oven. You wait another 15 minutes, and the cookies are still not baking. It is only after you look at the oven that you realize you did not turn it on. Most people are not turning on the oven but continue to put the ingredients in the oven. Change your patterns.

3.   The situation will get harder before it gets better, so go through the storm.

A friend of mine recently explained that a lot of our actions, as humans, towards others define our personal value. We attach our identity to the titles we are given which determines our value, our worth and what we believe that we deserve.

For two months, after a breakup, I was so emotionally exhausted that I took an emotional break. I not only mourned the relationship, but I also mourned the person I was in that relationship. I had given up hope and thought that I could not love someone like I loved them. It hurt to feel emotions. It hurt to give of myself to others. In those two months, I was at my lowest and I felt like I would never get to the other side.

Then, one day, I realized that I needed to put on my oxygen mask first. It was important for me to fill my cup first before I gave to others. I had lost myself in the life of someone else, and I had to bring myself back.

When the veil finally lifted, my emotions were more manageable. I realize now that I had to go through that darkness to get to the other side.

4.   You are the only one standing in between your unhealed self and your healed self, so get the fuck out the way!

I believe it is safe to say that we have made the decision to not take steps to change the life that we are currently in. It is also safe to say that we are the only ones that can change it. Every day we fight the battle of change. Do we, or don't we.

My favorite quote from Eleanor Roosevelt is "Do what you feel in your heart to be right – for you'll be criticized anyway. You'll be damned if you do, and damned if you don't." When I first came across this quote, I did not quite take it to heart. I lived my life, made mistakes, experienced a broken heart, and so much more. It wasn't until I started diving into my healing journey that this quote stuck out to me. No matter what I decided to do, I had a choice. I could do nothing, or I could do something. When I chose to do nothing, there was no change. I was in the same pit I had been in before and the hole kept getting bigger. But when I chose to do something, that's when the world of possibilities opened for me and change began to happen.

By making yourself a priority and being selfish, you start to see how caring for yourself helps those around you. The change in your attitude and mood, the confidence and the self-esteem that builds. Trust in yourself and the ability to know that it will lead you and those in your circle forward. All without compromising yourself. Being able to wake up every day and truly say "I love me and the person I have become for myself and those around me," is a gift. What version of yourself do you want?

5. Patience is truly a virtue and you will get more than you bargained for.

By consistently practicing and putting myself first in my healing journey, I have had to be patient, which in this popcorn society has been the hardest part of my journey and the most fulfilling.

Patience is about being kind to yourself and knowing that the process you or other people are going through is not an overnight experience. It is about knowing that any move you make, especially if done before its time, may hinder you rather than help you. It's about letting the growth take place and allowing it to settle in.

Patience is not about tolerance. Being tolerant is allowing the behaviors of yourself and other people to go on when they show no sign of changing it. You cannot change other people. They must want to change for themselves. You do not have to allow others to continuously disrespect you or your boundaries, disturb your peace, or dissuade you from the changes you seek on your journey and put it under the guise of patience.

Be kind to yourself. Give yourself grace.

Now if you've read my warning and thought "that is way too much to sacrifice," I understand. Go ahead and put down this book now, it may not be the right time for you yet.

If you've read these warnings and thought, well I'm already in some of these places, but I don't see the changes that you've described, then continue to read further. I am going to show you how I went from tolerant, upset, being emotionally hijacked, giving too much, accepting very little, overspending, and being stuck in a cycle that wasn't moving me forward to learning patience, being even tempered, giving the right amount of myself, recognizing energy exchanges, trusting myself, being confident and becoming financially healthy.

What are you waiting for? Turn the page and let's discover the one habit that will change your life.

Terms You'll Meet On This Journey

Spiritual & Energy Concepts

Chakra – This is an energy center that can be found on your body. You will hear mostly about the seven primary chakras including Root, Sacral, Solar Plexus, Heart, Throat, Third Eye, and Crown.

Chakra Alignment – A form of energy healing that allows you to balance the seven primary chakras for overall alignment.

Reiki – Reiki comes from the Japanese language meaning "spiritual life force energy". Life force energy is the natural energy that flows through all living things and connects us to one another. When this energy isn't flowing smoothly, someone may feel blocked, depleted, or stress – showing up as stress, pain, fatigue, or emotional imbalance. Reiki is a gentle practice of energy healing that helps our body activate its natural ability to heal itself. By restoring the flow of this energy, Reiki can bring deep relaxation, ease discomfort, and return balance to our mind, body, and spirit.

Practical Reiki Master – A person who has gone through training and attunement to practice calling in Reiki to help facilitate healing for another person.

Energy Healing – A form of complementary and alternative medicine that aims to restore balance and flow to the body's energy system.

Soul Death – An individualized feeling of letting the self you know of "die" to make way for the new part of yourself. The soul death is different for everyone. It can be the feeling of not knowing who you are, what you will do next, how you can function during your normal day, and the absence of hope.

Disconnect – The feeling of not being connected with yourself, your mind, or your body. The feeling of being out of place or not grounded.

Visualization – A method used to help you mentally feel, see, or experience something that has not happened yet.

Mindset & Mental Frameworks

Clarity – The flowing of thoughts, ideas, and creativity that happens when situations and ideas click into place.

Transformation – The change a person goes through allowing them to experience a different part of themselves.

Accountability – Taking responsibility for the actions that got you here and the life that you choose to live.

Consistency – Consciously and continuously choosing to move forward with an idea, thought, or action to gain results. This can be every day, every other day, every week, etc.

Coping Mechanism – A strategy or set of behaviors that are used to manage stress and/or deal with difficult emotions. These can be healthy or unhealthy habits.

Reframing – Changing the way you think of a situation in the moment as to not fall into the assumptions of the situation.

Recalibration – Bringing yourself back to a neutral state of balance. Understanding if a yes before is a no now, or if it is still a yes. And vice versa. Redefining your tolerance .

Healing Journey – The journey that a person takes to understand themselves and their past experiences to become more aware.

Focus Word – A word that encompasses your goals for the year so that you always have a way to track how you show up in your life. This is used in place of a New Years' Resolution or a list of goals for the year.

Emotional States & Patterns

Trigger – A situation that brings up emotions that within you from a past experience. Not usually emotions associated with the current situation, but how a similar situation made you feel.

Catastrophize – Continuously creating the worst-case scenario for a situation until it ends in death.

Insanity – Doing the same thing over and over again and expecting a different result.

Therapeutic or Coaching Tools

NET Therapy – Neuro-Emotional Technique (NET) is a stress reduction technique. NET is performed using manual muscle testing of the arm in combination with meridian access points located on the wrists and hands. This technique is used to pinpoint specific emotions, memories, and stress patterns stored in the body.

Muscle Testing – During NET, a practitioner will ask you to say a statement while they test the muscles of an outstretched arm. If the muscles test strong when a statement is true, your outstretched arm will not move. If the muscles test weak or inhibited when a statement is false, your outstretched arm will lower.

Support System – The people in your life that you choose to share your journey with and who have your back. These people can be your family, chosen family, friends, co-workers, mentors, etc. These people offer you support when you are in a time of need and you are able to reciprocate the same for them.

Boundaries – A guideline that you set for yourself to control your actions.

Reticular Activating System (RAS) – The filter for sensory information responsible for attention and consciousness.

Radio Silent Weekend (RSW) – A pre-planned weekend, Friday evening to Sunday Evening, where you walk away from the notifications, social media, and people in your life who seem to constantly need your attention. This can be done alone, or it can be done with other people who follow those same guidelines. The idea is to not have any distractions and give yourself some unfiltered self-care.

Reason #1

Because Changing Feels Impossible When Alcohol Has Been My Comfort Zone

How Do I Even Start Breaking Unhealthy Habits?

At the end of 2018, I started rewatching seasons of *The Amazing Race*. If you don't remember the show or have never seen it, it is a reality show where two-person teams travel all over the world solving riddles, gathering clues, and taking quizzes to make it to the finish line for the money grand prize. Every day, I would come home from my job, make dinner, and sit in front of the TV to watch strangers travel the globe. This tidbit would not have made it into my book; except I was watching *The Amazing Race* for six hours a day.

That's right. I had a dirty filthy habit.

If I didn't have anything else going on in my life at the time, I would not give this a second thought. However, not only was I married, and worked a full-time job, but I also had a business that I was trying to get off the ground and was not doing so great at it.

I was in my fifth year of being a network marketer and although I was making money, it was not as consistent as I wanted it to be. I had friends who were working this business full-time and were making a full-time income, and all I wanted to do was not have to sit at my desk job all day. In order to build a foundation to bring in a full-time income, I knew that I had to put more time into my business, but where would I find the time?

You guessed it… probably in those six hours a night I was wasting watching *The Amazing Race*!

The truth is, I had built a habit and routine of how I spent my days and although I wanted more, I would fall into the same pattern every single time. Over time, the habits we have created become automatic based off the cues that we give ourselves for an action or habit loop to start. For me, it was knowing that once I made my plate I was going to sit down in front of the TV. But how could I break this habit and start to put forth effort elsewhere?

When you begin to break a habit, you have to decide whether you are proactive or reactive. When you are proactive, you can see that there is a problem or issue that needs to be fixed before it gets out of hand, if it hasn't already. You decide to change so that you don't continue to hurt others around you, or yourself. It is a conscious decision to do something rather than respond. By being proactive, you increase your chances of breaking the old patterns.

When you are reactive, you respond to situations oftentimes without thinking. People who have not practiced being proactive are likely reactive in situations. People who are quick to act can make mistakes. Imagine you get into an argument with someone, and this argument results in hurting someone's feelings. In order to put the situation right, you decide that to make the other person feel better you are going to change your ways and never do it again. Sometimes when you do this, there is a temporary relief period where things are going great, and after a few weeks you begin to fall back into your old patterns and unfortunately do the same thing again. Does this sound familiar? When you are reactive, you increase your chances of falling back into the same old patterns.

I identified my pattern, and now it was time to be proactive and make a change. I set a goal for myself to cut out TV for 30 days. In my mind, this would give me more time to read, or work on my business. I knew that I had to make a change, and it had to be drastically different from what I had been doing. My business wasn't suffering, but in order for me to make it I had to actually do the work.

I created a foolproof plan. I was going to quit watching TV, cold turkey, and the only thing that was going to stop me from watching TV was post-it notes. The greatest technology alive! For 30 days there were two yellow post-it notes at the top of my TV. One of them I had written, "Go read a book" and the other one, "You should be working on your business."

Of course, there was nothing really stopping me from turning a blind eye to the post-it notes and turning on the TV except the commitment that I made to myself and the fact that I did not want to let myself down. It was that commitment that moved me forward.

Since I was doing this to build a business, I needed to quantify my goal. I wanted to earn $5,000 in my business in the next 30 days. My new habit loop: come home, make my dinner plate, go to the den, see my post-its, roll my eyes, eat dinner at the table, then go work on my business.

I have been to numerous conferences and learned a lot of different ways to be productive and grow my business. Now it was time to put some of those things to work. It was hard at first because I was fighting my urge to watch TV, and overtime it got better. As I worked on my business, I got more parties on the calendar. I started to bring in more money, and I made more than I had ever done in a month up to this point. In the first three months of that year, I would do more than $9,000 in sales and one of those months I hit my goal of $5,000 which was a huge accomplishment. The company even gave me a necklace that had a 5k charm on it.

I tell you this story so that you know that no matter what the habit is that you are facing and trying to quit, that it is possible with commitment and the desire to quit. No matter the decisions you make, you always have a choice. Your first choice is to react out of emotion, or you can be proactive and come up with a better way.

Sometimes we don't realize that the patterns that we are following in our lives are habits that we have created through trauma, boredom, or our peers. We don't realize that they have become an ingrained part of our lives and are hard to break. With a lot of our pattens and habits being automatic, it can be hard to figure out which ones are keeping us in the same position, and which ones are helping us find the person we want to be.

What do we do about it? How do we stop the cycle of the unhealthy and harmful patterns and habits that we have committed ourselves to all these years? Well, we start by making a change.

At the start of 2023, I stopped drinking alcohol cold turkey, and I was very proactive in my approach. I knew in November of 2022 that I was going to stop drinking, so I took inventory of what I was drinking, how I had access to it, and how I was going to keep from getting it. I had a wine subscription that came out of my check monthly. At any point in time, you could find a plethora of wine bottles in my house and recycling. I really loved wine. I called them and told them that I wanted to cancel my subscription. They told me that instead of canceling my subscription, I can put it on a six-month hold and start it back up if I wanted to. I told them that would be great. It allowed me to keep the bottles of wine I had accumulated over the last few months and give me time to decide if I really wanted to cancel the subscription for good. Task number one, done.

The next thing I had to do was not buy wine or alcohol from anywhere. That actually was not hard at all. I nixed wine from my grocery list and just like that, I was no longer a drinker.

Here is the thing, in order for you to see what is affecting your life and what changes you truly want to make in your life, you have to take inventory of the things that are out of place in it. Ask yourself, do I know what habits I should break? What is the recipe for, insert situation, that I keep using and it still turns out the same way.

When it came to drinking, I did not have control over my emotions, the things I said when I was drunk, or how to handle any hard situation because the first thing that I would think to do was drink it away. For you, it could also be drinking. It could be that you want to lose weight, but you know that you overeat or don't eat enough healthy foods. You want to do a fun run with your friends, but you can hardly walk up a flight of stairs because you smoke two packs of cigarettes a day. You may want a healthy relationship but find yourself with the same types of people that you have always dated who leaves you longing for more. The list goes on.

It is not my job to tell you what you have to do to change your life. It is your job to take an honest look at the situations, patterns, and habits that you have formed to protect you, and start to unravel the mess that has been created to see what no longer serves you. There is an underlying reason that you are in this position. Let's find a way out.

Before we make a list of habits that you want to change, or think that you need to change, I want you to look at your life and ask yourself, what do I like about my life and what do I not like about my life. I would suggest you get a journal, notebook, or open a Word document on your computer and take notes. This list is your life inventory. Having a list is a visual representation of all the areas that you would like to change or see changes in.

After you have completed this list to the best of your ability, it is now time to pick an area that you would like to change and make a list of habits associated with that area. Know that there may be a lot of habits within some areas, but we are only looking to change one of those habits for now. This list can be as small or as expansive as you would like.

After you make the list, we are going to review the list and rank them. When it comes to ranking the list of habits, we want to rank them from most impactful change to least impactful change. For example, I wanted to not be angry and have a healthier relationship with myself and my partners. If I were to list the habits that I had in these areas, it would probably look something like this:

Habits:
1.   Drinking
2.   Not talking to anyone about my problems except for my friends
3.   Continuing to repeat things in my relationship that I don't like
4.   I keep asking for things in my relationship and still see no change
5.   I am not speaking up enough about my needs or wants in any area of my life, job or relationships

Now, if I were to rank these habits and give them a value of 10 for most impactful, and 1 for least impactful, it may look like this:

1.   Drinking - 10
2.   Not talking to anyone about my problems except for my friends - 7
3.   Continuing to repeat things in my relationship that I don't like - 9
4.   I keep asking for things in my relationship and still see no change - 3
5.   I am not speaking up enough about my needs or wants in any area of my life, job or relationships – 8

Once you've ranked them, choose one thing that you believe would be the easiest to give up or change for the next 90 days.

Now that you have decided on the one habit you want to change, now we think about the question we want to solve for this habit. When I stopped drinking, I wanted to see if the meme that I came across was true. *Stop drinking for 90 days and see if you need it anymore.* I wanted to know if this was true. Would I need alcohol after 90 days of not having it? Now, we have to build up the things that will help me with this task and the things that will not. Do I have the willpower to go out with friends who still drink? If yes, no change needs to be made there. If no, I must stop hanging out in places where my friends go to drink. What are all the possible changes that can be made? Do I need someone as support to help me with this task? What are the first three steps that I need to take to start this journey? Then after you complete those three steps, create three more. Just like that child said when someone names all the things they had to do, "It's only three steps."

Once you have created a plan for yourself, it is time for you to take action. Start by working on step one which in my case was not to drink. It was by far the hardest step that I had to take and remember I did it all cold turkey. The next step, get rid of any open alcohol in my home without drinking it. The final step, go one day without drinking. Your steps will look a little different depending on what habit you are choosing to create. This is just a start.

Journal Prompt: The habit I chose to change or create is _______________ and this is why. Then write down the steps that you are going to take and how you are going to measure your progress.

In the television story I did 30 days. So why do I want you to do 90 days? Honestly, because that's where I started. There have been plenty of studies over the years that talk about how long it takes for a habit to kick in or how long it takes to break one. In 2009, Phillippa Lally held an experiment where 96 volunteers chose a habit of either eating, drinking, or an activity for 12 weeks to see how long it took a person to form a habit. The results: a new habit can be formed between 18 to 254 days, and the average number of days that it takes is 66 days. Ninety days is clearly more than the average, and by then you will know that the habit is formed. After 90 days of not drinking, I decided to keep going for a full year. There were other influences that kept me going, but I can say that the habit started to take hold.

Now that you have the habit that you are trying to change, write out at least three reasons why this habit is something that you want to give up. Besides a meme telling me to stop drinking for 90 days, I had my own reasons for not wanting to drink anymore. The first reason was to give myself a break. Out of all the years that I had been drinking, this was by far the worst it had gotten. I drank almost every day, and I didn't really have a "good" reason to drink. The second reason was that I thought it might help with my mood. I was angry all the time and could not figure out why. Although I did not act on my anger, I knew that it may be a contributing factor and when I was angry, I drank more. The third reason was that I started to not like who I was. I was cruel to others, and I wanted to be better. I wanted to not only treat others better but also treat myself better.

Everyone's reason for changing will be different. It is essential that you explore your why and how that will affect your progress. We will talk shortly about why your reasons are important.

After you have your reasons, the real work begins. What are the things that you can do to help yourself break the habits, keep on track and not lose faith in the process? Your life inventory is going to help you see the things that continue to repeat in your life and may have been the same for a long time. It is a reminder that the changes you are about to make will in fact make your new life inventory more fulfilling and different than what you are used to.

What are the ways that you can help yourself break your habits? One of the ways that you can do this is to find an alternative to the habit you are trying to break. When I wanted to stop watching TV for a month, it was reading a book or working on my business. When I stopped drinking, I found a supplemental drink option. I researched different mocktail combinations, and I bought sparking water and juice. Whenever I became stressed out, angry or had a strong urge to drink, I went to the kitchen and made a mocktail.

The interesting thing about habits is that until they are pointed out to us, we don't realize we are doing it because it has become so ingrained in our lives. Think about your morning routine to get to work. You wake up in the morning, get ready for work, eat breakfast while walking out the door, get in your car and then you're at work. Do you remember how you got there? What route did you take? The reason for this is that our brains find shortcuts to life that allow it to shut down and not be used as much, like the way you take to work. This is how a habit is formed.

Before I started this journey, I did not know the reason I overindulged in these habits. All I knew was that when I got irritated with a situation or wanted to escape my mind, I went to the fridge, grabbed a nice cold sparkling water and juice. I grabbed my wine glass because who said wine glasses are just for wine? And I poured angrily into my cup as I cursed whoever or whatever made me want to escape, and I drank down my mocktail with fervor. The action of it helped. The bubbles in my drink helped. It was not until later I found out my triggers which we will talk about later in the book.

The one thing that I did not think about was what do I do if the urge hit me to drink or to watch TV. What do I do if I want to fall back into my old habit? Know that the urge does not go away overnight. For the first few days that I stopped watching TV, I was irritated that I made this commitment to myself. I would make dinner and walk right into my den… I cannot tell you how many times my post-it notes "yelled at me". It was the same after only two days of not drinking, I really wanted to drink.

I think about the chorus of Linkin Park's 2003 song *Breaking the Habit* as I write this. They sing:

I don't know what's worth fighting for
Or why I have to scream
I don't know why I instigate

And say what I don't mean
I don't know how I got this way
I'll never be alright
So, I'm breaking the habit
I'm breaking the habit tonight

I had to break the habit. Now, we explore the why.

Why And Desire: How To Stay Focused

Your why does not have to be complicated. The trick is to make it simple and measurable.

In most multi-level marketing companies, or MLMs, owning your why is something that they teach you to do. You talk endlessly about your goals for your business and what you want it to look like. Then you create a plan, put that plan in motion, and watch the fruit of your labor. The same principles can be used when you are creating a new habit.

One thing that I have learned about myself and the people around me is that unless we want to change, we will not take the steps to do so. This is why having a personal why is important.

As a trauma survivor, I always tried to fix others and their situations. A friend or random person would come to me about their problems, and I would turn into Mrs. Fix-It and give them all kinds of solutions to help them with their situation. And geezus, you have to do these solutions right this instant in the exact way that I say!! I found out quickly that it does not work that way.

We all have our own paths to go and mistakes to make. You are not able to make a change until you make the decision to change, and you have a big enough reason to change.

Now, there are a shit ton of books out there about creating your why, so I am not going to go in depth about how to do that. What I do want to make sure of is that you know exactly why you want to quit or make the change.

When I started my 90-day no alcohol challenge, my why was very simple: I wanted to stop being a bitch all the time. I felt like I could not control my temper, and I was always on edge. I was not satisfied with my life and the relationships that I had. I hated the position I was in at my job, and all I could think of doing was escaping into a bottle.

Now, notice that I didn't say that I wanted to quit drinking because of other people in my life or because someone told me I should. You will have influences in your life that will make you want to change and those who support your change. Remember, in the short term, you can and most likely will make changes for the people you care about most in your life. For lasting results, your desire to change has to be for you.

To help you figure out your why in the next few moments, I want you to ask yourself: why do you want to quit your unhealthy habit or why do you want to change? Don't think on this for too long. Write down the first answer that pops into your head. Congratulations! You just found your why. Your why will change overtime, but we want to put feet to the ground and take those first steps to change.

As you start to walk on this journey, think about who you can bring along to be your support system. You do not have to walk this journey alone. This could be your family, friends, spouse, significant others, your chosen family, or a local group that you attend. It does not matter what that support system looks like. These people do not have to be making the same changes as you. They are there if you need someone to talk to or if you need a pick me up conversation.

Your support system is very important during your time of discovering yourself and changing your habits. My two best friends did not participate in the 90-day challenge, but they were there to talk me off the proverbial ledge when I felt like I wanted to drink... boy oh boy. They were such godsends.

On the day that I broke up with my partner, I called my best friend while sobbing uncontrollably. Even though I was the one who broke up with them, I felt so lost and broken about it. I told my best friend that all I wanted to do was drink and she said, "you can do that if you want... but you'll regret it." I laugh as I write this, but she was right. I was almost to my 90-day goal, and I would have regretted it instantly had I succumbed to my emotions, drank my sorrow away, for the moment, and didn't deal with the hurt and the pain I felt. Having people in your corner to cheer you on, reassure you, and letting you know what kindness and patience look like are great resources to have.

As you get started, talk to your spouse, significant other, roommates, friends, family and/or kids and let them know that you will be making some changes, that it is going to be hard, and that you need their support. People want to feel needed and connected, so why not let them know how they can support you? For example, if you choose to change your eating habits, you may change your grocery list to add healthier choices like vegetables, fruits, and low sodium products. For the people who live with you, ask them what healthy options they would like to always have in the fridge to snack on. You could also have each person choose a favorite snack that you always have in the house for them, and when it is gone, it is gone until the next shopping trip. These tiny changes could help your household manage their eating habits as well and curb their snacking but also support you in a small way.

Quality time is another great use for your support system. It was not until late November of 2023 that I realized that I needed more quality time with my support systems. This included my family and my friends. I had been focusing on myself and my healing journey that I felt as if I had neglected my friends and my family. I felt like I had not seen them in a long time and that other than major holidays, I did not really get to see my family all that much.

Think of ways that you and your support system can get together a few times a year to hang out and be there for one another. I once drove twelve hours, by myself, to see my best friend and spend time with her, her son and her mother. One thing that has been true over the course of history is that humans are not a species designed to be alone. We thrive on companionship, and we grow when we are around others. Continue to foster the relationships that you have with others and watch how your relationships grow.

When you are in business, there are a lot of groups, networking events, and conferences that speak about being in business for yourself, but not by yourself. There is alwats a group of people that you can go to, who have been through similar struggles, and can help you through the moments in your life that reflect what they have already gone through. It is a good way to make friends, have accountability partners and see that the obstacles that you face are not unique to you. Everyone goes through something and knowing that someone else was able to get past it and thrive is what you need to take that extra step, make that extra call, take one more break, and get back on your game. It is all about perspective and the people that you keep in your circle.

When it comes to your support system don't forget to nurture them. I know that I would not have gotten this far in my healing journey if I had not had people in my corner who loved and supported me. A support system, just like any other relationship, is one that should be nourished and taken care of. Not all the time can you be there for someone when you are going through shit, but when they need, you can be there for them just as they are for you. You will have the capacity to help them through their time of challenges. There will be plenty of times when you are there for someone in their time of need and that same energy will be reciprocated when you are going through something. Support systems should be balanced and reciprocal. In these times it is important for you to know what you need and be able to ask for it.

For your sanity, overall life balance and the health of your support system, I recommend taking regular trips and vacations, so that you can all get a break from normal life. There are approximately 46% of adults who do not use their paid time off from work. Our bodies were never meant to take on the amount of stress that we put our bodies through. And let's face it, most people think that they don't deserve a break or believe that they can't take a break because of the amount of "work" they have to do. The reality is the work will never be done and if you take a break the world will not fall apart.

As I type this, I am getting ready for a week-long vacation. I plan to put down my work for seven whole days and enjoy the sun with my best friend and her boyfriend. Prioritizing yourself, your mental health and your time is one of the best things that you can do for yourself. The one thing that I love more than anything is a break from regular life. I know that the things that are going on in my life will be there when I get back, but when I take a break and come back, I can think of a plan to work through and find solutions.

Go spend time with your family and friends. Take a trip together. Enjoy the time that you have on this Earth because we are only allotted so many years and we never know when that time will end.

When you have your why, and your support system, the how comes into play. How are you going to stay on track? How do I keep myself focused? Your why is going to guide you in every way to keep you steadfast in your decision. Creating a new habit and sticking with it is going to take perseverance and consistency. You are going to fight with yourself every day and make the conscious decision to keep going. Keeping your why in the forefront of your mind is essential.

A person who strives to be the best salesperson in their company can only do so if they have a plan. They know that every day they come into the office, they will follow up on emails, make 50 calls a day, contact their clients to check in, and make more sales. They recognize that to be the best, they have to be above average. Each person knows what they want to achieve, but they have to know that it is truly what they want, and they have to put in the work.

The events and changes that took place over the next year helped me to learn how to be consistent, create healthier habits, focus on my wants and needs, find better coping mechanisms and so much more. I let go of one habit, and my life changed before my eyes. Nothing in my life was the same. From the people I once hung around to the things that truly made me happy. Life felt less complicated. The decisions I made came easier over time. My view of others and the ways I showed up became clearer. I started to see patterns and that led me to more changes. I begin to ask myself: How can the changes I've gone through help someone else who is struggling with change? How can the changes I've gone through help someone else decide to start their healing journey?

Exercise & Celebrations:

Take some time once a week to contact one of the people in your support system. Catch up with them on the phone or in person. Go out to eat, drinks, or a paint and sip. Do something that you all will enjoy. Tell them how much they mean to you and how you would like your relationship to continue to grow. Explore ways to nourish each other and make this a routine.

During this time, celebrate your support system. Celebrations do not have to be a big party or a shoutout on social media. It could be getting them a card and thanking them for their support. It could be getting them a random gift because it made you think of them. No matter what it is, celebrate the people in your life that make you feel loved and alive. Never let them go too long not knowing how you feel about them and how happy you are to have them in your life.

The Phoenix Awakening: Soul Death & Rebirth

Changing is hard and it hit me like a ton of bricks after my breakup. I had no idea what I was in for, and I did not know exactly how to explain what I was experiencing.

In 2018, I hired a woman named Vanessa to help me build my coaching business from scratch. I have had many coaches and the reason I chose her was because of her no-nonsense style, and how she showed up authentically in her work and in her life. Later in 2023, I decided to go through the program again and in one of her videos she described exactly what I had gone through.

Vanessa explained that she had just moved, wrote her book and hated her life. She was at a point where she did not want to live anymore. She describes having a lot of disappointments that derailed her life. She was working too hard, she had disappointments around money, her relationships, and with God. In this time, she wrote a post about the long dark night of the soul death which lasted for several months, and it hit me. That was where I got this idea of my soul death. It was my lowest of low time in my life where I truly was disappointed in where my life had ended up, my job, money, and the relationships that I had formed. Nothing was where I wanted it to be and I was very unhappy.

The dictionary defines disappointment as sadness or displeasure caused by the nonfulfillment of one's hopes or expectations. That is exactly where I was: broken-hearted and left to pick up the pieces of the fantasized relationship I had created.

Vanessa explains that when you are full of disappointment it is a low vibration emotion, as you can see from this chart. There was no way for her to go around it, but to go through. She then introduces us to the disappointment exercise. This exercise helps you to call out your disappointments, feel the emotions behind them, and finally let them go so that you can move forward. When you allow yourself to process the disappointments in your life from a young age to now, the attachment to the emotion behind it does not last that long.

A picture of the emotional spiral.

After I listened to her story, I realized that when I ended my relationship with my partner, I went through the same thing. I felt out of place in my own body. I could only express that everything felt different or off to me. I was not my same bubbly self. I was not giving as much to others as I once did. I felt like I couldn't love again. I did not want to feel and to make sure I didn't, I cut out anything that could elicit an emotion which included TV shows, music, hanging out with friends, even spending time with my boyfriend. I felt immediately depleted any time I showed a smidgen of emotion. It felt like I was in a deep state of sadness. I had lost my zeal for life.

Here are two entries that I made towards the end of my soul death that dive into what I was feeling:

5/12/23 2:58 am

It hurts to feel right now. My heart is breaking slowly and cracking right down the middle, through each vein, through every vessel, The pumping has stopped and it feels like the love has gone away.

I know its there. It's still there. I feel a sliver of its light holding on. I can hear its whisper in the dark. It's a tiny light that shines, but it's there.

Right now it's dim from the pain and the hurt. It's nestled in a safe place for just me to hold. Giving it all away left me here and now I feel nothing, but something still lingers.

That little sliver of love, that little light, it will grow again. Time heals all wounds, and my heart is no different. I've always known what love is, but what does that look like to me.

This dim light is what I gave myself. I only left behind a little bit. It's certainly not what I deserve, so I'll nurture it until it becomes brighter. I'll continue to give it love until it fills my heart and heals it. Love is abundant and amazing. There should always be more and enough to give to self at all costs.

Soon that light will come out of hiding. It will show itself again and it will burn brighter than ever. Until then, hold on to that light. Nestle close and keep it warm and secure.

5/12/23 3:06 am

It hurts. It hurts to breathe. It hurts to move. It hurts to feel. My heart has never felt so exhausted out of love.

I've never felt this pain. Well maybe once, but it wasn't exhaustion. It was different. There was pain, but it was very different. That was more loss. That was a grief most know.

This… is not just loss. This… was grief mixed with loss, mixed with underappreciation, mixed with no reciprocation. It is the wall that falls and lets everyone in who shouldn't be there. It is no care given and no one to help.

It is blankness and sadness and loss and grief.

It's cold and jaded. It's dark and lonely.

Have you ever felt this type of pain before? Have you ever been so low that you felt blank? If so, you may have gone through a soul death.

My soul death lasted from about March 18, 2023 to June 1, 2023. In that time, I consulted with my NET Therapist, energy healers, and my talk therapist to figure out what was going on with me. During these sessions, the word that came up to describe what the feeling I felt was despair. The word despair means the complete loss or absence of hope, and it can also be found at the low end of the emotional spiral. At that moment, everything started to make sense. I had withdrawn from my Self and my emotions because I had lost hope.

During those 75 days, I did a lot of self-reflection, nurturing, and learning who I was to my core. It was a deep dive I didn't know I needed, and a process I am grateful for to this day.

On June 1, 2023, I wrote in my journal that I started to notice that my feelings were coming back. I started to feel like myself again. It wasn't until I started listening to music that fed my soul, 90's pop, that I noticed I had not listened to music or expressed any emotions that entire time.

Listening to my coach's video made me realize that we all go through dark moments in our lives and that they can last a moment or they can last a long time. Either way, there will be a moment when you break through it, but you must work through it. You have to go through it.

This breakup allowed me to understand what I was giving to others, how much I was giving to others, what I saw as my worth and my position in people's lives. Whether I played the role as lover, friend, or acquaintance, I started to realize that I was a person who gave my all to others and often, it was not reciprocated. I know now that the reason I allowed this to continue for so long was because I numbed myself to it with drinking. I used alcohol to keep from having to deal with the disappointments in my life, so they kept coming back.

Through this experience, I realize that the soul death is a recalibration. The soul death allows you to reflect on what has been working, and what truly has not worked. Recalibrating allows you to discover what we want and how we're going to start showing up in our lives and for others. It makes you realize the things that you are no longer going to stand for. I was at capacity in my relationship and when I left that relationship, I lost a piece of myself. I spent a lot of time giving more to people than I was receiving, and this forced me to find my balance again.

What did I want in my life? What did I like to do for fun? What am I looking for? I integrated into other people's lives and had not brought others into my world. I began to take myself out to dinner and go to activities by myself, regardless of whether someone went with me. I was no longer going to let someone else stop me from going out and enjoying life. I was gaining control of my time again.

I felt like a phoenix who was at the end of its life. I built up a shelter around myself and I burst into flames. I burned down every iota of who I thought I was, and I let it go. I reflected on my past and I decided to let that person go. I wanted better in my life and the only thing that I could change was myself. I rose from the ashes of my past as a new person and damn if I didn't feel good. This was my rebirth and although I didn't know it yet, there was still a long way to go. This was just the beginning of my journey, and I was ready for the ride.

Let's find out the other reasons you are still drinking.

Reason #2

Because I'm Scared Of Who I'll Be Without Alcohol

I'll Lose Everything

What are you afraid of? And once we figure it out, how do we move past it?

When we are changing from our old Self to our new Self, we feel as if we are changing everything about ourselves. We are fighting our urge to go back to comfort so that we can grow and understand our lives in this new space. I have come across a lot of people who either love change or despise it. Those who do not like change at all will say it is because they are afraid of losing everything.

To know what "everything" is, we have to first define "everything" for ourselves. Each person views the world through their individual lens and scope that they have placed on the world. Something that one person cares about with their whole heart; another may see as minuscule. Every person has a set of beliefs, values, and standards that they hold dear, and they may feel lost, confused, or even depressed without those things. You must ask yourself, what do you feel will be detrimental to your life, your existence, if you lose it?

When you begin your healing journey and start to see that there are things that need to change, it seems like your whole world is falling apart. Everything in your world represents the comfort that you are living in currently. How do you view yourself and the life that you live? Are you afraid to lose material things, people, or the image that you created to protect yourself? Most people don't know what to be grateful for, let alone what they could lose in their lives.

Take a minute to look at your life and ask this question: what do I lose if I don't change? Take inventory of the things that you have physically, emotionally, and mentally, and take stock in them. Ask yourself, do I have a home/apartment/living space? If not, how does that affect who I am? If you have a job, how secure do I feel in mt position? Will I be in this position forever? Is this a place to fill my time before I move on to something better? Dive deep into the things that you have and the things that you perceive to have. Once you have taken inventory of what everything is to you, look at all these things and ask yourself how does this serve me?

When people are afraid, they start to catastrophize their situation. Think of it as doomscrolling, except you see the doom in your life. When an idea pops into your head and you start to think the idea to literal death, that would be catastrophizing. This exercise is for my overthinkers to help you work through your situation from beginning to impending doom.

To start off this exercise, we take a situation and start the doomscroll. We work through every single scenario that we have in a situation and think of everything that could go wrong in that situation. At the end of the doomscroll, it ends with "then I die."

As you are working through this exercise, you will start to find new solutions to the problems that you are facing. Any thought, any idea, any situation, can be catastrophized, and those same thoughts have a solution that you have yet to see or act on.

Pull out your journal and let's start by making a list of what you feel encompasses everything in your life. That could include your home, job, friends, family, spouse, children, material things, etc. On a separate sheet of paper, I want you to break down each of these categories. In the home section, I want you to write out what it would be like to lose everything that is relevant to your home. Doomscroll through your home situation and see what solutions you come up with.

After losing her partner, Riley was working on getting her life back on track. She was in debt, her credit was not the greatest, and she was behind on her household bills. She desperately wanted to change, but she was in a situation where she knew that she could lose everything, including her home. When Riley created her list of the things that she could lose, it looked something like this:

Home
I could lose my home to the mortgage company. They could foreclose on my home, and I could live out on the streets. My credit would go way down, and I would not be able build it back up to get another home. I would be homeless.

All of my utilities would be shut off. Because I do not have shelter, I will not have anywhere to eat, lay my head, or protect me and I will die.

This list encompasses what was in Riley's mind. She then took each thought on this list and thought about a solution to each of those problems. For example, Riley wrote "I could lose my home to the mortgage company. They could foreclose on my home, and I could live out on the streets." She may write down:

I looked over my mortgage statement and realized that I am only one payment behind. I can call my mortgage company to see if I can make larger payments for the next two months to bring that balance to current. I can also talk to my mortgage company to see if they have any programs that may help me get back on track. I can ask the mortgage company how many payments behind I have to be for them to start the foreclosure process.

When people are faced with difficult decisions, they often stress out about the situation that is right in front of them and not how they can solve it. This exercise allows you to create a scenario that you know does not yet exist and take power from it. That way, you can look at it as a problem that needs to be solved before it gets bad. This turns the catastrophizing thinking into more of a solution-based conversation.

In Riley's situation, she has to look at not only how it will affect her if she loses her home, but also if she keeps her home. Maybe if she keeps her home she will not be able to keep up with her payments unless she gets another job, or maybe her home is too big, and she wants something smaller. There are many ways that changes can serve you in your life. You are making an active choice to change, so take it head on.

When you can figure out what it is that you are losing out on, whether it is everything or just a few things, you can make the changes to resolve your situation. Ask yourself questions like, how could I lose this if things in my life were to change? What would happen if I changed and lost a close friend, or who I thought was a close friend? How would that change my life? How would it make my life better or worse? You can take these things apart and take a deep look at what you may or may not be giving up if you decide that a change has to be made. Not everything is about losing. It is truly about what you are gaining.

Continue this exercise as you analyze the other areas of your life and look at what you could personally lose, like your mind, your life or even yourself. Take this time to think about the internal struggles that you may be going through and how that would affect your life. What would losing yourself look like?

You could be walking around like a zombie and feel that you are always on the "Struggle Bus", so what happens if you were to lose your present self and change who you were? Maybe you lose every friend that you have in your life and continue on the bus. Or, maybe you get off the bus and start to see that you can make new friends that fill your heart, mind, and soul. Some changes may take more effort than others but realizing where you are in life and then checking in with yourself to see where you want to go will help you see that changing is a great thing.

Here is a way of looking at it. Think of your earliest memory as a child. Do you remember how carefree you were about life and the things around you? The next time you're out, pay attention to the child walking down the street and stopping at every crack, flower, puddle, or toy. Notice how curious they are, what they want to explore in their surroundings and how they see the world. It is only as they get older that they start going to school, and paying attention to the situations around them, that they start to form a sense of who they are.

As we go through life, we draw on the beliefs and values that other people hold and how they might be useful in our life. We get into relationships with other people, either platonic or romantic, and we start to take on some of their beliefs and values, all the while getting further and further away from thinking for ourselves and keeping our beliefs and values in check.

Think about the times at work or in a romantic relationship when you decided that you wanted to change who you were to impress someone else. How natural did that feel? Did you question why you were doing it? Did you ever get exhausted after being "someone else" all day? That, my friend, is losing yourself. When you do this for a long period of time, you start to lose sight of who you are. When you lose yourself, you lose a lot more than just the material things in your life. You start to waste and wither away. You can lose your mind, your body and spirit. Sometimes you don't even realize that it is happening until it is too late.

Have you already lost yourself? Do you even remember who you are anymore? Do you know what beliefs and values you hold? Are your beliefs and values that of someone else's? Have you decided who you want to be? How do you find yourself again? How do you put the puzzle pieces of your life back together?

As you move through the process, remember that this is not an overnight thing. You will take these steps one at a time, and you will see progress little by little. You may not be able to recognize the old you, but you gained something more, your true Self. Never let anything happen to you that you would not want to happen to others. You would not believe how energized you feel after being yourself for just a little bit. It is like breathing brand new air. The only thing is that you have always had it, you just had to find it. No wonder you're afraid of losing everything, because that everything is you.

It'll Be Uncomfortable

I would like you to take a minute and do a visualization exercise with me. Imagine that you are in the dead of winter. A snowstorm is blowing in that night and all you can dream about is the hot sun melting the snow, beating down on your face and warming up your body. You dream of beaches and sunshine and how lovely it would be to be in warmer weather… then summer hits and its 85 degrees out, humid and sticky, and you wish for it to be cooler. How did you feel during that exercise? You may have felt uncomfortable when you imagined how cold it was outside, or when it was sticky and humid outside.

This happens to a lot of people when the weather changes. We know that every season the weather is going to change, yet we still have a moment of uncomfortable adjustment when it does. You know that it will be cold in the winter, and every time winter comes you wish for the opposite and ask why mother nature has to be so rude… You are probably laughing right now as I was when I wrote this. Because you know that it is true.

Just like the weather, people change. Whether we like to see it happen or not, they always do. For the most part, people want to stick with what they know and will justify their actions by saying "that's just the way I am". Some people believe that if they are inherently one way that they can't change, or that they don't have to change because they have created the person they are around those behaviors. Some people don't want to be different than they already are. Most people do not like being outside of their comfort zones, and for those people, change is a huge undertaking and extremely uncomfortable.

My ex-husband used to say that you had to be comfortable with being uncomfortable. At the time, I did not understand the words and how they fit into my life. I felt comfortable where I was and I did not want to change. I did not realize that many years later those words would come back to me as I vowed to stop drinking for 90 days and make changes in my life that were going to make me the most uncomfortable, I had ever been.

The uncomfortable part of changing was rewiring my body and mind to stop the habits I was so used to doing. For the first three months of the year, I changed my entire routine. I woke up at 6:30 am, took a lukewarm shower and did work for my business. For quite a while, that shit was uncomfortable as hell. I did not like waking up early. I did not want to take a lukewarm shower. I wanted to be cozy in my bed and sleep until 8:15 a.m. I wanted to take hot showers and do things the way that I had been doing them. So why didn't I continue to do the same things that I was doing every day? Why did I risk my comfort to be uncomfortable?

I wanted to shift my mindset and my attitude towards life. I wanted to feel better about the day I had, the work I created and feel like I was doing something productive with my life. I did not know if the changes that I decided to make would help my attitude, or if it would make me feel as if I was doing something in my business, but I thought that maybe… just maybe, this one thing might help. Every day, I woke up, meditated, worked on my business and felt accomplished, which would elevate my mood entirely in one month.

Here's the thing, you have to change the language that you use. Stop telling yourself that it's just the way you are and make the changes to be better. You do not have to stay the same person you were yesterday. You don't have to keep using the same excuses that you have always used. You can change at any time. You just have to be willing to do so. The first step is to decide that you will change, pick what you are changing, and then do it.

You can listen to hundreds of self-help gurus, but nothing compares to realizing that the only way you can change is if you act. You have already decided to stay the same and go through the same bullshit. Why not make the decision to take a different path? What is more uncomfortable: realizing that you are in the place that you were three years ago, or that you can change your life with one action?

Think about where you are comfortable in your life and choose what you are going to do to make it uncomfortable. Get out of your comfort zone and watch how your mindset shifts, your habits become healthier, and your attitude towards your life starts to change. Drink less. Change your friend group. Take yourself out on a date. Start creating the life that you want.

Change is uncomfortable, and I would do it again knowing that my life is very different from what it was five years ago. Start getting uncomfortable so that you can find comfort in the new life that you create and feel fulfilled in.

Everything Will Be Different

In 2000, Deborah Cox and Whitney Housten made a song called *"Same script, Different Cast."* If you have never heard it, this song is about a man who is leaving his partner for another woman. The two women have a conversation, and the partner who is being left recognizes the things that the new woman is saying. She tells the other woman that he told her the same things before and now he is leaving her. The song is a warning to the new woman that although she has her man now, it will not last long because he is the same person he was before. This is often the case in many situations. We go around saying the same things and doing the same things, and nothing ever changes. We get stuck in the same script.

The definition of insanity is doing something over and over again and expecting a different result. Changing is going to be scary, but I want you to think of your life as "Same cast, different script".

You are reading this book because the old script that you used to portray your life is no longer working and quite possibly has not been working for a while. We must change our internal script. Why do you need this drink? How long have you been using alcohol, food, or drugs, to numb your feelings, escape, or feel better? What is it that you really want your life to look like? What changes can you make that will shift the way that you go about your daily life?

What are you holding onto that you know no longer serves you? A relationship that no longer gives you fulfillment or you find yourself lost in their dream and what they want. A one-sided ten-year friendship, that you realize you no longer enjoy. Your negative attitude towards life and the people in it. You do not have to continue to be unhappy in your life. You get to decide what will make you happy. You may have never thought about it before but figure out what fills your heart with joy.

We all know that change is inevitable, and still, a lot of people feel that change is scary, and something that they want to avoid altogether. When I talk to people about change, it always amazes me how many people don't want to do it. Some of these people don't like the way that their life is currently, but if someone suggests that they change something, that is the something they avoid.

I have talked with people who say that they are scared that what they want will still be elusive to them, or that they worry about how the change will affect other people in their lives. Understand that when you change things about yourself it will affect those around you. It will change you into a person that you may not recognize, but that does not mean that the person you become won't be someone you enjoy. Not everything that is right for you will be right for others, but you have to realize that living your life for someone else will make you feel like you cannot fulfill your purpose. It will make you feel like an imposter to your life. People who are afraid of change are the people who have lived in a life that they deem comfortable and do not want to disturb the ecosystem of it. You may be happy where you are and not have to change, though this is not the case for a lot of people.

Over the years, a lot of my life has changed in many different ways. Some of those changes were because I wanted to and others because I had to. Take a look at what causes you discomfort with change and figure out why you fear it. You would be amazed at what you learn about yourself and that fear.

When you decide to make changes in your life, you are finding the person that you want to be. You are designing a life that fits the world that you want to live in. When you know who you are and what you want, the changes that you make will not seem foreign, but like a warm inviting hug.

"Well, that is all well and good, but I might not be the same after I change." My comment to that is that's the fucking point! The very action of changing is to not remain the same. Think about this: your taste buds, skin cells, and bones change on a constant basis. Your taste buds change every 10-14 days. Your skin cells, every 14 to 84 days, depending on age. Your bone cells change about every 10 years. We are literally wired to change.

Making changes and starting new habits will guide you to your ultimate goals and desires in life. This helps you to become the person that you have always wanted to be. The person who makes a choice and trusts that it is for them. The person who knows that they will positively affect those around them. The person who cares about how they treat themselves and others. Knowing what you do and don't need and/or want in your life will help you to find the peace and understanding that you are looking for. This alone will help drive your mission to understanding self, making consistent changes, and seeing the growth that is available in your life.

I cannot say that everyone is the same and that going through the same changes as someone else will yield the same results. We are all individuals and therefore have a different path that we are meant to take. Scientists have calculated that the probability of you or I existing today is 1 in 400 trillion! Every person has their own unique path to follow. Start from where you are right now and decide what you need to do for you, not what you think others want from you.

As a coach, I can tell you to do exactly as I did, but the timing may not be right for you. If you come to me and say that there are not enough hours in the day to get all of your tasks done, I will suggest that you start waking up earlier or staying up later to complete them. Most people will hem and haw about it. Most people do not want to upset the routine that they already have going, but those who know that they want to change will take the leap and do it.

I got up early to make content for my Tik Tok, learn consistency and get my business running. If I did not find the time to make that change, I would not be writing this book. Find what works for you. Find the change that you are most comfortable with and go for it.

I watched a movie on Netflix where a spy team used AI to calculate the odds of a plan working out for them. The main character was good at accomplishing the mission at hand and liked to take risks, even when the odds of completing it were low. In any situation, she knew what the risks of the mission failing were, and she took any chance to complete the mission, even if her odds were less than 5%. Her team members were more cautious when it came to taking chances, but she was ready to achieve the goal by any means necessary.

Have you taken risks in your life? What happened when you did? How did that risk affect your path? People take a lot of risks in their life, and how they view them in accordance to their life is important.

There are many things in life that people want. They want to make more money, or they want to inspire the masses by writing a book or making a movie. Yet not one of them takes a risk in changing their actions to get it done. When I started writing my first book, I talked about it for years before I wrote one word. When I started writing the book, it took me six years to get it done. For those six years, I talked about that book every chance I got, and I never knew when or how it would be published.

When we take a risk, we do not know every outcome. We can take a guess at what will happen, but we also have to decide if the goal that we want to achieve is worth the time and effort that we put into it. I took a risk writing my first book. I published it in 2021, and here I am, two years after the publishing of my first book, writing a second book about something completely different. We take risks every day in life. What do you have to take a chance on to make the changes you want to see? What are the risks and the disappointments that you face? Most people will have to ask themselves, is it worth it to put myself out there to get the things that I want? The answer will always be yes. It is completely worth it. You never know exactly what will happen, but you know that it will pay off. It pays to do things differently.

Chapter Exercise:

This chapter talks a lot about what you lose when you go through changes. In this exercise, I want you to look at the positive areas of change and how it will impact your life and those around you.

Take out a piece of notebook paper or your journal and draw a circle in the middle of it. In this circle, I want you to write out all the changes that you want to achieve in your life. These can be big or small changes, so write out as many as you can. Once you have completed your list, I want you to draw another circle on the outside of that one. In this circle, I want you to list how these changes can affect the money you make. Then, the next circle will be your health and well-being. Then family and relationships. The last circle, future possibilities. If your paper is not big enough for circles, you can also do this exercise as a list.

Some people have to see the changes that they are making and what that looks like in different areas of their life. This will help you to assess the risk, understand what you will gain and have a positive outlook on change. Keep this list somewhere you can look at it and remind yourself why you are making changes. Be not afraid.

Reason # 3

Because I Feel Stuck, And Drinking Feels Like The Only Escape I Have

Where Do I Start?

Feeling stuck can be the worst part of changing. It is a state of not knowing where to go next or what to do. You can feel stuck mentally, emotionally, physically, or spiritually and oftentimes we don't know how to get out of it. This is where people give up before they even begin because the ever-looming question is: Where do I even start?

Over the last eight years of healing and working on myself, I would suggest starting with your mind. Everything in this world that has been first created in someone's mind. They thought of a problem, came up with an idea, and it took shape in their mind. Then they took action to make it a reality.

When I decided to ditch New Years' Resolutions, I wanted to have one big goal that I focused on instead of five. I thought to myself, what is one overall goal that I can work on that will help me to accomplish not drinking for the next 90 days and to help me grow my business in the next year? That is when consistency popped into my brain, and I ran with it.

Your mind is the house where your world is created. Thoughts are energy and they can create or break your reality. Have you ever started off having a great day then one "bad" thing happens and it completely derails you? What about when things in your life are going smoothly and all of a sudden you start thinking about what happens if? You ruminate on it for a while, until you are obsessed with the thought of it and then one day... BAM! It happens! The other shoe that you thought was going to drop, finally does, and all you can say is I knew that was going to happen. Psychologists call this phenomenon a self-fulfilling prophecy and can be linked to the Reticular Activating System (RAS).

The job of the RAS is to regulate behavioral arousal, consciousness and motivation. Simply put, your consciousness becomes open to the things that you think about. For example, when Riley was looking for a new car, she went to the dealership and started test driving cars. She settled on a Nissan Rogue. After she bought it, she started to see the car everywhere. At the grocery store. Driving next to her on the freeway. Why? Do you think it's because people around her all of a sudden were getting the Nissan Rogue? No. It is because her mind homed in on that specific model of the car she now has, and she notices it more. The only thing that has changed is what her mind is focused on.

The Secret and *The Game of Life and How it's Played* are books that talk about how you can create your reality to activate the RAS before you get the thing you want. The stories in these two books focus on the methods that other people have used to get their dream job, their dream car and their dream home. I highly recommend you pick them up. One story that sticks out to me is about a woman who wore black because she always thought of herself as a widow. Due to an unforeseen accident, her spouse passed away and she in turn became a widow. That is the power of the mind. Whether good, bad, or ugly, your mind is a powerhouse that has the ability to repel or attract the things that you think about. Use it wisely.

Sherry and Dave were newly married and decided that they wanted to buy a new home. They both had different ideas of what they wanted in a home and could not quite decide what they wanted together. Sherry wanted a home where she could entertain guests and have enough space for their families to visit. Dave wanted a large house with a lot of space and wanted to have it designed to his specifications. Both knew that their house existed but were not sure where they were going to find it.

One day, they found what they thought was their dream home. It was 2,500 square feet, with a good-sized backyard. The whole house had an open floor plan with intercoms in each room, and the bedrooms were amazing. It needed a little bit of love and attention since the carpeting looked like it came straight out of *Austin Powers*, but it was exactly what he was looking for. Sherry was okay with the house and was not quite fixated on it like Dave, but they decided to put in a bid.

Over the course of three months, things with the home kept getting pushed back. The real estate agent had a complete change of heart and didn't think they should put in a bid on the home. Dave's friend, who did renovations, was taking forever on the new plans for the house. Eventually, she made the executive decision to stop the process and back out of the sale of the home. She felt that something crooked was going on in the background, and the delays were making her rethink the process. She looked for a new real estate agent and told Dave to have his friend stop the planning on the home. Dave was not happy and did not like that they had to give up their "dream" home but understood Sherry's hesitation with moving forward.

With their new realtor in tow, they went to visit a handful of homes that they thought would work out. One of the homes was nice, but the rooms were small, and the space was kind of cramped. There was one home they visited that had space, but the home was infested with fleas. As they searched and searched for a home, nothing seemed to be right. Dave would compare all the floorplans to the "dream" home and felt that they were never going to find the right space for them. The house wasn't open enough, or there weren't enough rooms. It wasn't exactly what Dave was looking for. So, the search continued.

One day, Sherry went to Dave and told him that he had to let go of the home they had bid on previously. She told him that for the Universe to give them what they were looking for; he had to stop comparing every single feature of the new houses they visited to the "dream" home. She knew that any home that they went to visit would not match the same feel, look and size as the other home, but she also knew that there was a home for them. She needed Dave to believe it so that the Universe would open up and show them the home.

Over the course of a few weeks, Dave worked on letting go of the home and finding the right home for them. Then one day they received an email from the realtor. A new home had come up on the market, with the space, about the same size and had an even bigger backyard. The price was also a lot cheaper than the dream home. Dave saw the email first and with excitement sent Sherry a text message with a picture of the home and told her to have the real estate agent put in a bid. Sherry was taken aback by how quickly he wanted to move on the home and asked if he wanted to see it first. He said yes, and to also have the real estate agent put in a bid for it. Sherry sent a text to the real estate agent and told her that they wanted to put in a bid and made sure that she set up an appointment to see the home as soon as possible.

They did a walkthrough of the home and talked with the women of the house for three hours. They learned a lot about the home and what the owners wanted from the buyers. As they walked out the door, they told the real estate agent to put in a bid on the home immediately. And to their surprise, they won the bid! The biggest surprise was finding out later, from their agent, that they were the only ones who bid on the home. Apparently, there was a mix up in who the bids had to go through since the owners had switched agents, so the other offers were not going to the right agent.

Sherry and Dave wanted a home. They searched, visited multiple homes, and found a home they liked. The process to that home fell through, and they had to start over. When they focused on what was theirs and how they could get their home through divine processes, the Universe provided. They got the home that they wanted and didn't have to fight for it, because it was divinely theirs.

Think about a time when you thought things were not going to work out, and they did, they just did not work out in the way that you expected. When you change your area of focus and the mindset behind it, you will start to see things change around you. In order for them to get to "their" home, Dave had to let go of what he wanted first so that he could see other opportunities in front of him. If he had not let go of the home that he desired, it is possible that he would not have been able to see the value in the home that they ended up with. It may not have been the same in every way, but they did get more than they bargained for, and the price was in their budget, unlike the other one.

Consistency and Mindset Exercise: Choose one thing in your life that you would like to change or have. Write a story about what it feels like to have that item or change. Make sure that your story includes all your senses. What do you see? How do you feel? What do you smell? What do you hear? What can you taste? Then once you have written this story out, read it often. Whether it be once a day, once a week or once a month. Keep this story in the forefront of your mind and as you move through life, see how you start to align with that story.

As you continue to feed your mind and rewire your brain, nourishing your body is the next step. When you stop drinking, you start to notice how your physical body feels without it. Your brain starts to clear up as if you had been living in fog. Your face starts to clear up and starts to get thinner. Your body stops feeling bloated and you begin to notice that your body is becoming firmer. You may not realize at the time that it's alcohol, but eventually you start to see the connection. It is not about the bad things you put into your body, but about the good things, and the actions that you take to make sure that the one body that you have is maintained and healthy over the course of your life.

Now, I am not here to tell you how to take care of your physical body with workouts or healthy eating recipes. It is more than that. It is about feeling comfortable and safe in your own skin. Finding ways to take care of yourself without the destructive tendencies you once had.

Coming from someone who has experienced childhood sexual trauma, there were times that I did not always feel the most comfortable or safe in my skin. Nourishing and listening to your body can help you see issues before they arise so that you can take preventative measures and not just reactionary ones. You want to understand how your body moves, how it feels and how to tell that something is off. Once you start to pay attention to your body, you will start to notice what it needs or even what it craves, and you can answer the call.

When I stopped drinking, I was depressed and at a loss for what to do with all of my emotions. Although I had felt my emotions before, I did not actually deal with them in real time because I had found a way to ignore them or bottle them up. In the first three months, I had gone through a crash course in my emotions. During these times, it was hard for me to sit and meditate. I thought back to when I was preparing for the Spartan and how it really helped me to focus my energy on working out. So, I decided to start running and it worked like a charm.

When I got restless, upset, or started overthinking a situation, I would go for a run. I did not have a set amount of time I would run; I just ran until I felt like the energy was gone. I used physical momentum to help me think and it worked. Now, you may not be able to run, or maybe you don't like to run… which is fair. You may find peace walking, playing basketball or tennis. Remember that you only get one body. Take care of it in every way that you can.

One thing that I learned in this year of healing, is that it is important to be connected to your emotions. Emotions are the window to your soul. Understanding your emotions can help you to empathize with others and help you gain acceptance of the deeper parts of yourself. I know a lot of people who do not do well with emotions, and that can be for multiple reasons. Maybe they don't know them very well or have not been taught how to feel emotions. For some, having emotions makes them uncomfortable. Maybe they were taught that having emotions makes you weak or feminine, which could not be further from the truth.

Our emotions do not dictate our weakness and it sure as hell does not dictate whether someone is masculine or feminine. Emotions are a normal part of life and how you handle them will determine how you deal with situations that come along. No matter if you hide your emotions or have them out loud, learning your emotions will be a great way for you to connect with yourself and others around you.

When George and Patrice started dating, they decided that they would have a monthly check-in. During these check-ins they would talk about how they thought the relationship was going, how they felt, and things they needed to discuss in their relationship. After each check-in, they would ask each other for three feeling words. They could describe how they felt about the conversation, or how they felt overall. They did not have to explain their emotions, although they could if they wanted to, but it was important that they knew where each other were emotionally. To keep from giving feelings like happy, frustrated, angry or sad every time they had a check-in, George decided to bring in the idea of a feelings wheel. It gave them more specific feeling words to use and opened up the doors for them to truly understand what the feeling was instead of a "baseline" feeling. If you look at a feelings wheel, you will see the happy category has words like joyful or content. The sad category has words like depressed or guilty. The feelings wheel helps you to become more specific about your feelings and tie emotions properly to how you are feeling.

I came across a Tik Tok video one day and a woman was talking about a situation that she experienced. Her friend asked her how she felt, and she wanted to use upset, but it didn't feel like the right word. Her friend helped her to find the actual emotion that she was feeling, and it turned out that she felt embarrassed by the way that this person had treated her. Sometimes anger or sadness is not really anger or sadness. It could be that you are feeling vulnerable or glossed over. If they hadn't looked up other words and feelings, she would have used upset and not gone any deeper to the underlying trigger. Yes, there will be times that you are angry or sad but understanding other feeling words can help you to home in on your triggers.

As I start to understand my feelings more, I realize that I want to control my emotions less. I explore my emotions and dig deeper to find out what it is that I really feel under the initial feeling. The next time an emotion starts to come up, take a minute and explore it a bit more. Think about the last time you were angry. What was the situation that happened? Can you think of any other emotions that you felt at that time? Was it anger? Was it frustration? Was it confusion? Explore those emotions and when you find the emotion that fits, ask yourself why that emotion came up? Is it connected to a previous situation? How was that situation handled? Then once you have the emotion and the connection to the initial situation, breath through it, feel it, and let it fade away. This helps you to process emotions. Once you are done, see how you feel. Do you feel lighter? Do you feel that you have a better grasp on that emotional trigger? You are doing good.

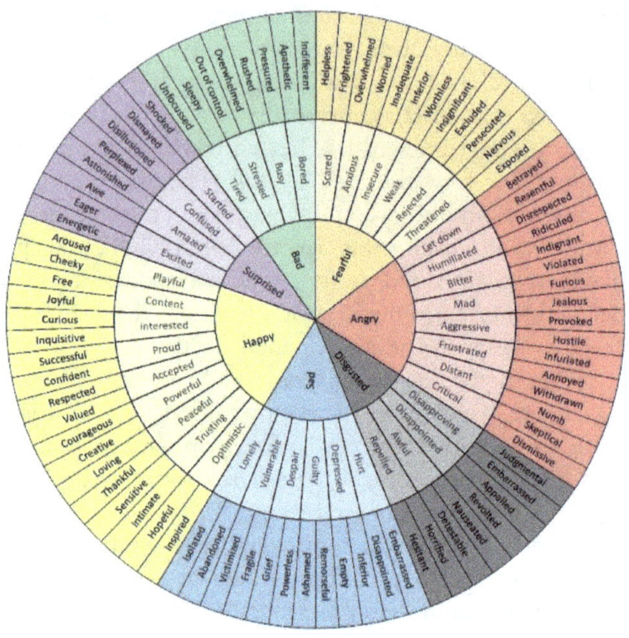

A Picture of the feelings wheel.
https://feelingswheel.com/

Now, we have talked about the mind, body and emotions, let's explore how you can connect all of these parts in your life.

Alternative Healing

My first experience with an alternative form of healing was while I was a sexual health consultant. One of our leaders, Christina, had team meetings at her mother's home and one of them was a wellness night. We got awards for our accomplishments, and she had people there who did tarot readings and Reiki, a form of energy healing. Although I was not familiar with Reiki, it was something that intrigued me. As I sat waiting for my cards to be read, Christina came to me and said that because I had always been the first one to the meetings and the last to leave, she was gifting me a Reiki session. I was so excited!

I met Meg who told me a little bit about Reiki and how it worked. I lay on her massage table, and she asked me if there was anything that I needed relief from. As she told me the different types of healing she could do, I opted for general healing because I did not have any pain. Meg began her session, and for 15 minutes she worked on my energy. I could feel energy moving around in my body, like waves. I could feel my body slightly swaying, although I was completely still. It was a different and cool feeling.

Years later, I started my trauma release business and was writing my first book. It was then that I decided to use Reiki to help release stagnant and traumatic energy as a part of my coaching. I knew that Reiki was the right modality of energy work for me. Christina and Meg became my first teachers.

After my first Reiki session, I subscribed to Meg's email list and for a few years, my inbox filled with her emails about taking classes to become a Reiki Master. It never felt like it was the right time to do the classes and the money didn't seem to be available for it. I was in the middle of my marriage falling apart. I was working long hours in my business and at my full-time job.

After my ex-husband left, I went to therapy, started working on myself and healing from my trauma. It was not long before I decided to start my energy healing journey. I wanted to clear my energy first before working on other people's energy. It should be noted that you do not have to heal before you become a Reiki Practitioner. It was important to me that I heal and release my own trauma before I started to help other people heal. I had a lot of doubts, shame, guilt, and hurt that I wanted to release before I felt comfortable with helping others and performing energy work sessions on them. After many sessions for myself and more healing, I was ready to start my journey. I followed my heart and my path, and the opportunity came about a year and a half after my ex-husband left.

As I sifted through my emails, I found another email from Meg about an upcoming Practical Reiki Master class that she was holding. The timing felt right this time. I knew that this was my chance to start.

At the time, a friend of mine and I were discussing Reiki and wanting to become an energy healer. We had been talking about energy work and meditation, and she mentioned she would be interested in taking the class as well. So, we looked at the website and got all the information we needed, pricing and all, so that we could sign up.

As before, I did not quite have the funds to do the course, however I was determined to make it work. I was sure I could come up with the $95 for the first class, so I signed up. Even though I was no longer a sexual health consultant, my friend was. She was actively hosting parties and about a week before the class was set to start, my friend told me she had a party but not a lot of on-hand products. She asked me if she could take some of those products with her and she offered to give me a percentage of the money from my product sales, so that I could pay the class fee.

That day, she went to her party and sold just enough of my products for me to pay for the first class. The rest, as you would say, was history. I was able to pay for the subsequent classes and become a Practical Reiki Master.

After the very first class, I started to perform Reiki on others, and very quickly realized that I had found my calling. I enjoy energy work and how it helps others, so I decided to have it as part of my practice and coaching. I knew that people would be interested in a different approach.

It has always fascinated me to learn the different ways that you can heal. Over time you will find that you know exactly what your body needs to heal. When you become clear, you start to understand who you are at your core and the things that you need to bring yourself back to center. This is why it is important to get to know yourself. Knowing who you are, what you like, what you don't and how you move through the world can lead you into a place that will help you heal faster. You never know exactly what you will like until you try. Healing is not always going to be fun; it does take hard work and consistency.

Finding And Understanding Self

Over the years, I found a multitude of ways to nurture and give back to myself. I found ways to show myself love, to reconnect and to find true understanding of the person I am. There are many methods out there that can help you piece together your true self. One method that helped me sort out the majority of my trauma, connect my mind, body, and spirit, and gain clarity in my life was a chakra alignment.

After experiencing Reiki and getting chakra cleanses, I learned about energy, the importance of clearing the chakras, and how that change in energy can help you understand yourself. It was years later that I happened upon *Journaling the Chakras* in a bookstore that put me on my right healing journey.

My ex-husband and I were not on the same page about our relationship, and we had basically become roommates. There were periods of time that we would go without speaking and when we did talk, it would end up in a fight. I remember wanting to get out of this phase of our relationship. I was hopeful that it could be fixed and all we had to do was change, talk, or focus on the right things.

At the time, we were close to his married cousins who were religious, and they suggested a few books to help. Although I did pick up the books they suggested, I quickly realized they weren't what I was looking for. Being an avid reader and self-help girlie, I thought there had to be another book that existed that would give me more answers, more techniques, and more skills to help me fix whatever had been broken within our relationship that was less religious based. I honestly didn't know what I was looking for as I wandered around the bookstore. For 30 minutes, I searched for what I thought would be the perfect book to help me "fix" my marriage. When I found it and read the first two pages, I realized that the change that I needed to make was in me.

That winter, I started on my first chakra alignment. I started to see the patterns in my life, work, and relationships. I had been walking through life making the same mistakes in different situations. The results of my patterns were the same and since I never paid attention to them, I was falling victim to them every single time.

This process starts at the Root Chakra which allows you to build a strong foundation. The right foundation needs to be sturdy and level so that the structure being built on top of it does not crumble. Think about the amount of work that would need to be done each time your house fell, and each time you fix everything except the foundation.

Out of the seven major chakras, the Root Chakra is responsible for grounding, stability, and security. During this stage you learn where you are insecure, how you handle situations and what values and beliefs you hold. You begin to look at the areas in your life that are not well put together and where you could stand to build a better foundation for yourself. As you peel back the layers of your life through mediation and journaling, you can see that there are some things in your life that are important and others may not be needed anymore.

Here are some unedited journal entries from the Root Chakra alignment I did in 2018, 2022 and 2023.

October 25, 2018

I like my body, but sometimes I do think that it could be better. I have not let myself go, but I also have not been keeping up with it either. It is a good body and I love it. It feels good as well. I love being in my body. It is nice to look at and it is mine.

I feel like sometimes I do not really give my body much love. I am so busy seeking that physical attention that I forget to love on it myself. I will do that sometimes, but not all the time. I don't feel like I am just dragging it around, although some days I am lazier than others.

When I was growing up, after being molested, I kept my body under wraps. I felt like people or men just wanted me because I had a body. Before I had sex, I kept my body hidden from everyone, even my mom. I was a prude and I was protecting it. After I had sex, it was almost like I opened up a door to my sexual beauty and never looked back. Being molested shaped my prude behavior. In the same step, sex took me out of it.

Now it is almost like I want to revert back, but also I don't. I don't want to be a prude. I believe I should be able to express my body and have people be fond of it, but also keep my wits about me and let them not deter me from the truth...

I love my body and how it looks. I don't need the thoughts or attention of others to know that. I am secure in that thought. How can I give myself a huge hug and continue to tell myself how much I love me? Everyday. Te', I love you! And that is not because of everyone else's thoughts of you, but because you are me and I am you and I am awesome! I love you!

As I hug myself, I can feel that amazing love for myself and I get teary eyed thinking that I could not give that to myself for so long. I believe that I will grow to love and nourish and take care of my body more. It is the only one that I have. Let's keep it amazing!

Where my root chakra should be, I feel a pressure. Almost as if it is full or overfilled with energy.

January 25, 2022

In today's root mediation, I am being called to write about my foundation and security. When I first began this journey in October of 2018, I thought that my foundation was pretty rocky. It seemed to start out strong, but overtime it seemed to crumble underneath me. As I went through my journey, I began to rebuild my foundation with me in mind. It was a good thing that I did because things in my marriage were falling apart and it seemed I only had myself in the relationship.

Losing that marital foundation made me feel lost and like I was a failure. Then he left. It was a crazy turn of events, but I felt like I had some of my shit together. I had started over and rebuilt. It was completely tough, but I had never been in a situation where I had to rebuild so many pieces of myself.

At this point in my life, my foundation is still a bit unsteady, but I am literally growing and building as I move on. My foundation is being built on my principles as my own person and not who people want me to be. In actuality, my foundation is stronger than I had before.

As far as security, I am working on building that in all areas of my life. At the moment, I am looking at financial security and how things in my life can be easier once I start to save and prepare.

I have always wanted to do that and truth be told I had before, but now I am making it a reality. Things are coming together and as much as I am excited, I am a bit terrified, but I am doing it anyway. Life is about fear. I cannot let it continue to paralyze me.

I have a home. I have a car. I have a job. I have a passion. I have a great support system. I have wonderful partners and I know what I want.

There had been times, even as of late, that my foundation did not feel steady. I think I just need to really ground myself often and look at the things that help me see that I have truly built a new foundation. I've fixed the holes that I had and mended the cracks. Things are now way better than they were before. So much better.

March 26, 2023

Today I did a Root chakra yoga with mediation. Surprisingly, I feel more grounded than the last two days. I realized yesterday that I am emotionally exhausted. I have been giving so much for many years. It has been just tiring. Realizing that I am making changes and really working on doing better for myself than those around me is super fucking hard! Lol.

Right now my heart is at a crossroad. What do I do? I've started on my grounding piece and that has brought me here… to find my security and rebuild my foundation.

At the beginning, I knew that this would elicit changes. I was not sure what that would look like, but I needed this time to truly ground and reevaluate.

Bringing myself back to rest, back to center has caused some turmoil, but not anything I know I'm not able to handle.

I am not sure where to go, but I know that one of the things I need to do is find my boundary. What is it that I truly want and will not allow. There are so many things that I can think of that messes with my current state of thinking. It amazes me that I literally have waited this long, but I know I have been working on it.

The last three months have been rough, in the aspect that I went against my boundaries. Now it's time to trust myself and know that the decisions I make are exactly what is right for me and not anyone else. The way that I am treated will be with respect and if that is not met in any capacity, I'm good on all fronts.

This is for friends, friendships, all of it. I cannot allow myself to feel unprotected and unloved in a way that I would NEVER do for myself. That is not ok.

Building this love for self and getting back to me in this moment is probably what I need. How do I want to play this?

I feel like taking an emotional rest while I do my chakra healing will be a good idea. Emotional exhaustion is the worst I feel. I want to show love and self-care and be with people who reciprocate the energy I put out and that had boundaries and all that. Wow, to make sure I bring that to the table and keep those conditions.

First and foremost, I love me, so anything that goes against that does not belong. It no longer belongs. Set the stage for what is about to happen. I also just noticed that it's been one week without any type of sex. That's today. This will be some interesting grounding work and chakra experience.

As I went along and learned more about the chakras, their meanings and how they connect to the mind and the body, I started to see where I had imbalances, not only energetically, but also physically, emotionally and mentally. I started to see how my life was topsy turvy because I was in fact topsy turvy. I did not know what I wanted or who I was anymore. I had lost myself in the relationships that I had been in, although I told myself time and time again that this would not happen. Understanding why I fell into those patterns was important to me.

The chakra alignments that I have completed have taught me the importance of connecting the mind, body and spirit. Each of them can function independently of one another, but in the end, they all work together to make one cohesive journey.

You do not realize how disconnected you are until you start doing the work. When you start to reconnect with yourself, it is like greeting an old friend. You know who you were, and the situations that you have been through, but you feel so removed from the person, your body, and your mind, that you have to relearn the most trivial things about yourself. Through yoga, pole fitness and meditation, I was able to reconnect to my mind and my body. I didn't realize I was missing the soul piece.

There is no right or wrong way to reconnect with yourself. Choose a method and begin.

As I started to reconnect with my true self, I did not recognize her. She was not who I had been before. She did not like the same things, and she did not act the same way. She was very different. I knew that it was mostly from her life experiences, but being unrecognizable was hard. I could have been lost forever, but instead I chose to become someone that I could be proud of and happy to be. I came to the realization that the person that I created was not the true me, it was an image of me that I no longer needed to survive. I no longer wanted to live in a world where I felt trapped by my circumstances. When you connect with your Self, you will find a world of freedom that you never knew existed.

One thing that I have always said is that healing is not linear. There is not a first step, a final step and then you're done healing. The changes that people make in their life are not the same as the ones I made nor the same as anyone else. You will discover what you need to make your life better, but you have to start exploring what that is.

Chapter Exercise:

Decide right now what it is that you want to focus on in your life. Decide on the methods that you will use to reconnect with your authentic self. Do you want to start yoga, meditation, energy healing, NET Therapy, or dance? What do you feel you have to change in your life? Who do you have to bring in to support you? What will help you connect your mind, body and soul?

Make a plan to start today. Find a class to go to or watch some YouTube videos on it. Learn what makes you feel good and how that feeling can help you make the changes that you so desperately seek.

Your life will remain stagnant the more you keep holding back and doing nothing. Open up to the world and the abundance around you and see what you can create.

Reason #4

Because Chaos Feels Safer To Me Than Peace Ever Has

Scheduling Peace

When I decided to make different choices in my routine like getting up early and engaging in activities that made me happy, everything in my life changed. Whether I was making a Tik Tok for my business page, or reading a book, I started to find peace in the early morning moments before work. These moments helped me to build on what I knew could be true: I did not have to live in a world of chaos every single day.

When I look back at where I was in April of 2023, I was creating a sense of peace that I had not yet experienced and for four years, I was struggling to get back on track after my marriage fell apart. I was so busy trying to survive my life that I was no longer living it.

In the hopes of getting out of the financial bind I was in when my ex-husband left our home, I started a full-time job with a law firm 15 minutes from the house. I knew that it would save me money on gas and on parking, but I did not think about how this change would play right into my need to survive and take my licks on the chin.

In my first three months of working at that law firm, COVID hit. Not only was quarantine kicking my ass, but I also worked myself to the bone every day. We had never been through a pandemic like this before, so we didn't know how the courts were going to deal with the virus. Every day, I worked late and anything the attorneys asked for I made sure that I could accommodate. They offered endless hours of overtime, and I took advantage. I was only making about $39,000 when I started and considering I had been a paralegal before, I knew that if I proved my worth, they would give me more money. I did not know how much damage I was doing to myself and my mental state and in less than two months, I burned myself out.

The day that I realized that I needed a break was at the five-month mark. I was working on a task when one of the attorneys came up to me and told me that a pretrial statement was going to be late. She told me that she understood that we had been working hard, and if I am too busy or need help to draft the statements to ask for her help with it. She did not raise her voice. She did not berate me about it. She simply informed me. I apologized for the oversight and let her know that it would not happen again. After she walked away from my desk and I sat there for about five minutes, I told my co-worker that I had to take a break and that I would be back shortly.

I left the office and went to my car. I climbed into the driver's seat, and I cried. It was the first time that I had felt overwhelmed to this degree, and I questioned if I was doing the right things in my life and job.

I knew that I was working too much and too hard. I felt like I couldn't stop. When my best friend told me I was working too hard and that I needed a break, I wrote it off and told her that I was okay and that I had to keep going. The writing was on the wall, but I did not want to see it. After that event, I talked to my therapist who suggested that I take a week off work to relax and get my head together. She even said that she would talk to my boss to let him know that it was important for me to take this time. I quickly told her that I could do it and I would request time off.

I was worried about asking for time off. After all, I had only been there for five months, but I had been killing myself to make a good impression, making money to literally keep food on the table, and honestly, I was exhausted. So, I walked into my office and let my boss know that I was overwhelmed and burnt out and that I needed to take a week off work, and it had to be immediately. I didn't know what he was going to say, but surprisingly he was receptive. We created a plan and list of things that I would complete before taking off the time, and he approved it. This began my journey of looking for peace in my life.

I heard somewhere that people who do not know peace cannot understand those who have found it. Right now, I want you to take a couple of minutes and sit with yourself. Relax every muscle in your body, take three deep breaths and truly feel your Self. Now, I want you to answer this question: What is your idea of peace? Use all five of your senses. What do you see? What do you hear? What do you smell? Can you taste anything?

How does the world feel around you? Take a moment and write down everything that you think of.

As I sit here and type this, the image of peace that comes to mind is the middle of the forest. Just me, the trees and the flowers. I can hear animals and birds as the wind blows the leaves up above me. I feel the soft patch of earth underneath my body as I lay down to nap and feel the soft, warm breeze on my skin. I can feel the warmth of the sun beaming on my face through the leaves and the smell of the waterfall nearby.

Take that image of your peaceful place, or you can use mine, and think about how that makes you feel? Do you feel calm and happy? Do you feel content and restful? These are some of the words I use to describe what peace is for you. Peace feels serene and relaxing. It is possible that not a lot of people experience peace because we are caught up in the hustle and bustle of life. In the lives of people who drink, the familiarity of chaos brings us comfort, but now that you have an idea of what peace looks like, how do you get it or create it for yourself? To begin, you must find out what peace is to you and how it will fit into your current life.

As I continue through life and talk to people about what they are searching for, I believe that people are searching for harmony. They want to know that their life and their work go hand in hand. That they can do it all without it causing them stress and having peace of mind. Harmony is the merriment of energy that comes together and works well together. That is what I was searching for.

To create peace and harmony within your life, schedule time in your day to do so. This is a simple way to make a commitment to yourself to do what in your world makes you feel peaceful. This can be early in the morning before the kids get up, or it can be right after you get off work before putting dinner on. It can be daily, weekly, or monthly. No matter how you plan this time, do it for you. Giving time to yourself is a gift and should be a priority. Don't let anyone take that away from you. During this time, sit down with a pen and paper or calendar and start to plan out what you want your day, week, or month to look like and schedule time to relax in your peace.

When you start to fill in your schedule, start with your major engagements first and calendar them. For example, put on your schedule the times that you work throughout the week. Do not forget to put in your commute time, if you work outside your home. Then block out mealtimes, mostly breakfast and dinner. Lunch may be covered in your work schedule, but you can block it out if it helps. Now think about other activities that you want to include in your schedule, like a hobby or sporting events for the kids. You want to make sure that your schedule looks realistic. Make sure you pay attention to the engagements that you have. Weekly date night, soccer practice for the kids, work functions, etc. Some people have a side hustle that they are working on. Don't forget to block out time for that. What about exercising or family events? You can also fill in wake times, bedtimes, reading times, literally anything!! And don't forget to block off time dedicated to creating peace.

Continue to work your schedule until you get it the way you want it. It is not going to be perfect, and you want to stay flexible. Sometimes your day will not play out exactly how you have planned, but you want to make sure that if you schedule an hour walk and something happens that you can't do it at 6:00 p.m. as planned, you find another slot in the day to get it done. Creating a schedule helped me to say yes to the things that I wanted to do, and no to things that I didn't want to do or have time for. It was a lot easier to decide what I was going to do in my days and weeks when my schedule says that Tuesdays are free and clear versus Wednesday when I had a full day of events planned.

When you create your schedule, make sure that everyone who needs to see your plan can and are involved in some way. My best friend and I talked almost every day. When her son wanted to spend more time with her, she created a schedule for her and her family so that they could do just that. She designated Tuesdays to family movie nights and Fridays to family game nights. Sharing this information with friends and family also helps them to know when you are available for time with them as well. This is the perfect way to start creating boundaries.

If you have a family, make creating a schedule an activity. There will be days for everyone that will be different due to work, school or extracurricular activities. Keep all of this in mind when you are creating your schedule so that you can still be present within yourself and with others. Remember that scheduling your activities and events is equally as important as scheduling time for yourself. Do not forget to set aside some quality time for you. You will thank me later.

Chapter Exercise:

Create a space in your home that will help you to think about peace. It can be a room in your home that you don't use often, or a corner of your home that you feel at peace in. Once you create this space, put on your calendar when you will use the space, how often you will use it and how you will use it.

Boundaries

In 2022, I hosted a Survivor's Empowerment Summit that featured 21 amazing coaches and therapists from around the world. During this 14-day summit, I interviewed women who had dealt with trauma, created programs, written books, and used a variety of methods to help people like me overcome trauma. As a gift to the attendees of the summit, I created a three-day workshop so they could learn more about what I do and how I could help them. It was called the Boundary Building Workshop.

When I began my healing and trauma release business, one of the major things that my clients were having difficulty with was how to create boundaries and enforce them, especially with the people that they were close to in their lives. The Boundary Building Workshop taught people the difference between boundaries and rules, what a healthy boundary looked like and how to maintain them. It was a very informative workshop.

So, what is a boundary? A boundary is a guideline that you set for yourself. They are meant to help guide you through your feelings and protect you in situations that make you uncomfortable or may not be right for you. Most people confuse boundaries with rules and will use them interchangeably. The big difference between them is that rules govern other people's actions, while boundaries govern your own.

Boundaries can be physical, emotional, or mental and are meant to help you keep your peace and mental health in line. As you think of boundaries and rules, think of rules more like laws. When you go over to your relatives' house and they have that one room that no one is supposed to enter, that is a rule. Another rule would be taking off your shoes when you enter someone's home. A boundary guides you on how you will behave when an uncomfortable situation happens.

Growing up, my youngest sister didn't mind receiving hugs. As she got older, that changed. She didn't like to be hugged by anyone other than her children and on occasion her partner. She let everyone know that this was a boundary. I have a friend who has a boundary surrounding the type of people that she will associate with. When I talk about boundaries, I let people know that boundaries are walls that are being built around themselves and that wall has a door. The person that has the boundary is telling you what they will tolerate and in what capacity. They are built to keep people around and to help you build trust in yourself. People who get upset that someone has set boundaries are often people who felt that they let them have open access to them and now they feel like they are being shut out.

Charlene had been dating someone on and off for years and realized that there were things that she did not want to continue in that relationship. She not only had conversations with him about what she wanted and how she saw their relationship but also decided that she would stop interacting with him in ways that were not congruent to the relationship she was looking for. When he noticed that she had changed, he told her she was acting "different" and was upset at the way that he was being treated. She set a boundary by telling him how she wanted to be treated in the relationship, and if the situation did not improve, she would move accordingly. He did not feel that he was treating her differently than he had previously, but she no longer wanted to deal with how he was treating her. In this case, he became more disrespectful and treated her like she was no longer special to him. Eventually, she let him go his own way. She decided what type of relationship she wanted with her partner and made a choice to not allow others to treat her any different than that.

Creating boundaries helps you realize what treatment you do and do not like from others and most importantly from yourself. After one of my breakups in March of 2023, I was thrown into my soul death. During this time, I involuntarily created a wall around my heart to protect myself from giving any more of myself than I already had. I knew that it was time to repair, rebuild, and recalibrate. I honestly had no idea what I was doing, but I had to take a hard look at what I needed to give myself and how others fit into my life.

During my recalibration, I decided that I needed to rebuild my boundaries through a zero-tolerance method. Instead of letting people in, I kept everyone out to repair my barriers. I allowed people to treat me however they wanted to for so long because I was afraid to stand up for myself or I was afraid that I would lose them. In order to find out who I wanted in my life and how I wanted to be treated, I took a drastic step. By resetting my boundaries, I was able to gauge my personal tolerance levels and how I interact with people in my life. I started to see that some people could stay, but others had to absolutely go.

When you create boundaries consider what values and beliefs you hold. What do values and beliefs have to do with boundaries? The values and beliefs that you hold help you to create the world around you in the way that you want it to be. Some of the things that you value could be time, positivity, love, and family. You also have certain beliefs when it comes to family, religion, politics, and other topics. Values and beliefs are formed over your growing years and continue to grow as you become older and walk through the world. When you know what those are, you will create more solid boundaries. You do not have to go as far as I did when I created my boundaries but take some time and evaluate the ones you have already.

People not only have issues with creating boundaries, but they also do not know how to enforce them and maintain them with the people that are in their lives, especially the ones who are closer to them. If you think about it, we have people in our lives that can get away with murder, figuratively of course. Then there are people who we don't allow to get away with the same thing. This is due to the relationship that we have with that person and often the excuses that we make for them. Plenty of times I have seen people talk down to a family member. The people around them defend this person's actions by saying, "Oh, they always talk like that," or "that is just how they are." We may never know why this person spoke like this to them, but what we can gather is that the person who is being talked down to has either not set a boundary or believes they deserve it.

Maintaining a boundary once it is created can seem like a daunting task. As a duty to yourself, you now have to tell people that they are not treating you the way that you want to be treated, and that you may have to leave that situation if the treatment does not change. To help enforce and maintain boundaries, my clients create an action plan for when someone violates their boundaries. When you are just starting this process, it may feel like you are trying to change the person that is behaving in a certain way. Remember, you are not there to govern their actions. If your boundary is to be talked to respectfully while having a conversation, and someone says something to you that you deem condescending, the first part of the action plan can be to let the person know that what they said is hurtful and you don't like the way they have spoken to you. You can then let them know what the next step in your action plan is. Maybe your next step is to walk away or leave the area if it happens again. If the action continues, you take the next step. When you stick to this action plan, you start to gain confidence, and trust in yourself more. You are teaching yourself to listen to your body when you feel uncomfortable and get out of that situation.

Here is a small warning, because I want you to be prepared for backlash from any person that you will take or have taken this action against. It is not always easy in situations like that, but in others it may be. If you have an encounter at a party, or when you are at a family reunion, it may be easier to walk away. Always use these tips when you feel that you are going to be safe afterward. If you are in a situation where you do not feel safe or in a domestic violence situation, please seek help so that you can get out of that situation safely.

If you're ready to go even deeper, I did an entire episode on boundaries with the *Forgive and Thrive* podcast and I didn't hold back. I

talked about the boundaries we set, the ones we let people bulldoze, and the ones we didn't even know we needed until someone crossed them. This conversation is real, raw, and uncomfortable in all the ways that force you to look at where you've been giving people access, they no longer deserve.
Take a listen here:
https://open.spotify.com/episode/51vJTXY3vGaxTvdRFyVKeI?si=CT BSIWZeQemjUFH3pu_PIw.

Radio Silent Weekend

Finding peace and creating boundaries were not an easy task. For many years, I had at everyone else's beck and call, and somehow, I forgot how to give back to myself. I forgot how to put my oxygen mask on first, so I took the steps to do exactly that.

When my husband left at the end of 2019, I started to see a therapist early the next year and I started to think about what I needed to give back to myself. How could I show up for myself? How could I make myself feel loved? I had just gotten out of a four-year marriage where I felt as if I was giving a lot of me with nothing in return.

Now that he was gone, I felt like I couldn't take a break from anything, especially from work. I needed to make money to keep the lights on, but I also felt that the salary that I was earning was not enough. In the time that I worked, it gave me less time to care for myself. I ignored my emotions and how I physically felt so that I could just barely survive. My life had been a rollercoaster of ups and downs, survival and fighting. At what point could I relax? How could I become less overwhelmed with life and the reality of people needing me 24/7? The constant barrage of social media notifications, emails, and text messages started to add to the stress. I wanted to be there for others, but how could I do that when I wasn't even there for myself?

Then, one weekend, I decided I would put my phone on silent and walk away. You heard that right. I needed a break, and I knew that it had to be drastic.

The rules were very simple: I would turn my phone off from Friday at 6:00 p.m. to Monday at 7:00 a.m. Absolutely no phone calls incoming or outgoing. Absolutely no social media. Absolutely no text messages to family, friends, or partners. I would take the time out to relax and be with myself for a weekend. And thus, Radio Silent Weekend, or RSW was born. To make sure that the people in my life would not worry, I told them when RSW was planned. They were very supportive of the idea since most of them knew I was going through a lot and by keeping them informed, they didn't worry when I didn't answer my phone.

The people in my life are used to me going off grid. One time, my group chat with my family wasn't working and when I asked one of my sister's if she noticed, she said "I thought you were going Radio Silent for a while." In shock, I said "For TWO MONTHS?"

For the most part, Radio Silent Weekend's take place at my house. I decide if I want to stay inside or if the weather is nice, if I want to camp out in my backyard. One time, I did RSW over Labor Day weekend and set up my tent in my backyard. That weekend I stayed outside, read, painted, started writing this book, and enjoyed nature. I went inside occasionally to eat, shower and use the restroom, but other than that… I enjoyed my time outside and away from everyone.

If I plan to leave my home or do RSW elsewhere, I will let my friends and family know. Over the years RSW has evolved and I sometimes will allow specific people to know that they are able to join me during RSW. The same rules apply, but this means that I get to have company. I will say that in all the time that I did RSW no one has taken me up on that offer.

For some people, this would probably be a hard task. I know people who cannot leave their home without at least one electronic device on them. If I could, I would leave my phone and my watch at home. I already leave it silent every single day.

The whole idea of not doing social media during RSW is to know that the world will still move without you. It is getting control of FOMO (fear of missing out) and taking your life back. I am pretty sure that one of the last RSW's I missed Jimmy Buffet's death. I have no idea how that happened, but the price I pay to get some kind of peace. Sarcasm intended.

The ultimate goal of Radio Silent Weekend is to relax and decompress without feeling like you have to be on alert every single second. There are a lot of times where I need to get out of my own way and take care of myself. I plan self-care tasks like reading, art, video games, NAPS, you name it! I am ready to do it. We are inundated with emails here, notifications there. There is never a time when things are just still, so why not intentionally create those moments to relax and help calm our nervous system? I honestly believe that all the notifications from our cellphones have created anxiety in most humans.

RSW made me realize that people will contact me, but I do not have to answer every text, phone call, email or social media alert right then and there. It can wait. Usually, if it is important, the person will call you or they will tell you what is going on in a text.

Technology has built a way for us to get instant gratification. We want everything right now, whether it be healing, groceries, or transportation. Almost anything can be summoned at the push of a button. Think about how you got this book. Did you go on Amazon and purchase it? Or did you get up, put clothes and shoes on, grab your keys, drive to the bookstore, search for it, pull out cash, pay for it at the register and then go home? I bet you chose the easier, more efficient way. We have gotten used to just sitting back and letting others do for us. There is nothing wrong with that. I encourage you to do what you feel is best for you. However, if you want to see change in your life, you are not going to be able to just push a button, and make it appear. You will have to take the time and do the work.

Chapter Exercise:

Plan a Radio Silent Weekend for you and your family. According to whatsthebigdata.com, the average person spends about five hours and 24 minutes on their phones. This of course can vary between ages, gender, and country. To help your family decompress from their screentime, pick a weekend that works. Preferably when everyone will be home, or even on a vacation. Think about what you want to accomplish during this weekend. Do you want to have more family time? Are there projects that you would like to work on together that have been neglected? Do you just want to have a weekend with no electronics?

I would suggest finding a place to put the phones so that there is no access to them. I would also suggest turning off the phones, if you believe that the silent setting is not enough to curb the craving of checking your phone. You can do this with smartphones and tablets only, or all screens. Let everyone know the plan and get started. This exercise will help you to become closer to your family and help you find other activities that you can do that do not involve the screen.

Reason #5

Because Complaining Is Easier For Me Than Healing

Bitching & Complaining

When life gets you down in the dumps and you feel low, what do you do? Do you stand up and fight? Or do you bitch and complain about it to your friends, family, or anyone who will listen? They weren't lying when they said misery loves company. For all the whiners, criers, and complainers in our lives, this rings true. If that is you, you may want to pay close attention.

As I walk through my journey and see how people handle their situations, I realize that some people idolize the "struggle." My ex-husband was like that. He would talk about how we had to suffer before things got better. He talked about being oppressed as a black heterosexual cis man. There were times that I would sit and listen to him talk and think, "This is exactly why you are where you are in your life." Then I would tune him out. I didn't realize until later that this was his narrative and it sure didn't fit what I wanted in my life.

He glorified the struggle and made everything about oppression. He always had an excuse for why things in his life weren't working out, why he didn't have this job or that job, and why his business wasn't growing despite the "work" he was putting in. He complained about how certain people in the video industry got more accolades than he did because of their race, gender, and sexual orientation. For my own sanity and peace of mind, I stopped listening to the "poor me" drama that he was living in.

Now don't get me wrong, do I understand that there are people who have it harder than others? Yes, I do. However, I also believe that we create our own realities. My ex-husband continued to push this idea that he was not able to accomplish anything because he was black, yet we have plenty of examples of how that is not true. The worst part was that he would try to drag me into his "poor me" drama. He wanted me to "suffer" like he "suffered," but I would not submit to that dialogue. There are so many people addicted to the "struggle" of life, and are willing to bring others down with them, just so they are not alone.

After moving from Cleveland, one of my Facebook friends made a post announcing that she was moving back. She was not happy about the idea and wanted to share with those in her friend group her woes. I looked through the comments and found that one of her "friends" had commented, "it couldn't be me, but good luck." My initial reaction to this was "Wow!!" Can you imagine your friend being so blah about something that you have to do, and it makes you feel even more crappy about having to do it?

I notice that in order to keep you in the same cage as them, people feel that they have to bring you down or if they can't have it, neither can you. This is called crab mentality or the crab-bucket effect.

While out catching crab, the sailor puts crabs in a bucket. As a crab is placed into the bucket, they realize that the walls of the bucket are too high and are not able to get out. Over the course of the fishing trip, the sailor continues to put one crab after another inside the bucket. As the bucket fills up with crabs, some of them try to escape. When the other crabs see that they are trying to get out, the others drag them down so they can't. This will continue to happen until the crab gives up and doesn't want to try to escape anymore. If the crab does not give up and it continues to try to escape the trap, the other crabs will kill it.

Some people can't stand to see others get ahead. Like you, I know many people who just love to bitch and complain at every step and drag others into their misery. On the flip side, I know others who love it when their friends go for their goals and dreams and achieve them. Find people who will continue to motivate you and support your dreams, not the ones who bitch and complain about how you made it out and now are too good for them to try to keep you in the same space.

When my ex-husband was going through his personal development phase, he introduced me to *The Game of Life and How it's Played* by Florence Shovel Shinn. Her book talks about manifesting and changing your life completely. She discusses the idea of bitching and complaining as having a good old-fashioned chat. She explains that having a "good old-fashioned chat" is talking about the old days and how things used to be. Something that a lot of people like to do. There is no thought of the future or what you are currently doing to improve your life. She suggests having a new-fashioned chat where you talk about the things that excite you or the things that are coming up in your life.

I know that stopping bitching and complaining or making the changes you want to accomplish aren't going to happen overnight, but this is your moment to start practicing. When you complain, you are perpetuating the narrative that you already created based off of the previous experience you had. I noticed that when I stopped complaining about the harm and "damages" that other people were doing to me, I was able to see what the underlying issue or trigger was that caused me to react. How would you feel if you could kick that to the curb and start brand new? The trigger that once set you off will no longer affect you as much. When you complain, you are putting yourself at a low frequency which will counter all the things you've set out to achieve. You can't say that you are a millionaire but complain about being broke. Ask yourself, "what would a millionaire do?" My best friend and I talk about the problems that we hear come up in people's lives. We hear all the time that struggling is part of the path, but who says that must be so?

People are going to complain about things that are going wrong in their lives. Things in life are not always perfect and when we get the chance to release that burden, we do.

What about all the good things that happen in life?

After I got married, my friendships started to change with some of the women who were in my bridal party. After not talking for a while and expressing that I wanted to see her, one of my friends came to me and wondered why I never talked to her about the good things that were going on in my life. At the time she asked this, it did not seem that I had anything good going on in my life. Yes, I had just gotten married… but right after the wedding I got a cornea ulcer that led to me not being able to see out of my left eye for nine months. I became depressed and did not want to do anything that involved going out. Things in my marriage seemed to be going off the deep end, and I felt that I had nothing happy to talk about. When I look back on the situation, I completely understand what she was talking about.

In the days after I graduated from college, I called myself the damsel in distress friend. I would only call on people for help if life was down the shitter and I saw no way out of it. I would be in a dark place, and I would only call on my friends when I couldn't pull myself out of it. When I did have something good going on in my life, I tried to include them as much as I could, but the reality is that it was not enough. I was not a terrible friend, but I didn't know how to be a good friend when things were good.

There will always be days where you have a "bad" moment, but that does not have to turn into a bad day. Be mindful of what is happening around you and how you can change a bad situation into a good one and make it worth it. If you wake up in the morning and stub your toe on the leg of the bed, look at that as just a moment. Some people will carry that throughout their day and no matter where they turn, it seems to go wrong. First, they stubbed their toe. Then they spilled coffee on their suit. Now, they are late for a meeting, and it goes on and on until the day is "ruined." Do not exchange that energy for the life you are living now. This is what makes healing so unique. It is not about only thinking positively all the time. It is about taking a moment to breathe, reframe your thinking, and choosing to make your day and life better every step of the way. At first, it is hard as hell. You are not used to changing your thoughts from negative to positive at the drop of a hat. Start off with one negative thought a day. As you start to move on and realize that ruminating on that negative thought will not change anything, then you start to see that it is useless. Change the vibration of your day.

I always tell my friends that once we bitch and complain about a situation, let's find a solution or let it go. Express your emotions, process them and move on. Don't dwell on it every single second of every day. As you continue to bitch and complain you will start to see how your energy shifts from good, to bad, to worse. That is the opposite of where we want to be.

When you start to understand what you want in life, you start to see that the things you complain about don't matter much. Sometimes we feel that the situation we're going through will never end, and most people will dwell on it and get consumed by it repeatedly.

Animals and humans will seek shelter during a storm so that they don't get caught in it. Some avoid it and others wait for it to pass, but not the buffalo. A buffalo will see a storm on its path and will continue to move through it until it gets to the other side. The buffalo understands that to get to the other side of the storm, you must face it head on. Go through it with the rain in your face, the thunder rolling and the lightening flashing. It will only last for as long as it takes for the clouds to roll over. If you continue to avoid it, you are prolonging the inevitable. In *Meet the Robinsons*, Lewis' friend, Goob, was mad at him for years and it manifested into anger, hatred and shame. It was the only thing that he thought about and before they fixed the past, Goob was heading down a dark path. How long are you going to dwell on those things and let them fester?

The Words You Speak And Think Make A Huge Difference

Have you ever seen Practical Magic? If you haven't, I am about to spoil a scene for you. There is a scene where the school kids come after Sandra Bullock's daughters chanting "Witch, witch. You're a bitch." The eldest daughter points her finger at one of the kids and starts to say, "I hope you get," and Sandra Bullock's character tries to put her finger down before she can finish her sentence. Her daughter fights through, lifts her hand and points her finger at the kid and says "…chicken pox!" Then when Sandra says "Oh, she doesn't mean it…" her youngest daughter says, "you know she did, mom." And guess what? Later in the movie you see the kid walking around town with chicken pox. This movie represents how powerful words are and how to use them wisely and only as intended.

Scientists say we have more than 50,000 thoughts a day. There is no way that every single one of them is positive 100% of the time, so you teach yourself how to use your vocabulary to your advantage. Speaking positively is a skill that can be built. It takes time and patience. How does one know what to say and when to say it?

When you are learning to stay positive, one of the techniques you can use is called reframing. When you catch yourself thinking negatively, you pause, think a different thought, a more positive thought, and shift it. Let's say you are in the middle of creating a piece of art. You have a vision for what you want to put on the canvas. As you add more glue, paper and color, you start to think that it doesn't look exactly like what you pictured in your mind. You start to curse your "gift" and start putting down your work. A slew of negativity flows in, and you stop. You close your eyes, take a deep breath, and say to yourself, "Stop. Your art is your art. You are not competing with anyone. You are simply creating a version of what you see in your mind. It is beautiful and it will look great." You then continue to work on the project until you complete it.

Using positive language and reframing your negative thoughts can be a huge change for your life and for the people around you. Not only do you get to see what it is that you have to offer, but you also get to see first-hand how common it is that people do not use language in a positive manner. It may be common for you to hear people talk about a situation as if it is happening right now. I'm not perfect! I still do this sometimes. The brain does not differentiate from experiences that have happened in the past and that are happening right now. You may know the difference, but your brain will replay a scenario as if it is happening over and over again in that moment. The same thing happens as you speak, when you use low vibrational words like want, I could have or I can't have, your brain finds ways to make this a reality, and it keeps you stuck.

There are a lot of tricks to being positive and the most popular one is "fake it 'til you make it." This is a trick used to help you get out of your comfort zone. It helps you smile more, become more confident and do things that you didn't think that you could do. For most people, the problem is the faking it part. How do you know what positivity looks like if you feel that you have never had it? All you can do is mimic what you see, and that can take you down a different set of spirals.

For you to move a mountain, you have to first believe that you can do so. To be positive in your life, you first have to say the positive things, live a positive life and feel the positive emotions. Using a method like visualization can help you get in touch with the feeling that you want to have. You will discover ways that you can have the happiness that you always dreamed of. As you change your mindset, you see where you want to go and how you can get there. Why continue the same path that you have when it has always left you feeling alone, down and like you have nowhere to go? Take a different road. The definition of insanity is doing the same thing over and over again and expecting a different result. Why would you want to keep doing that? Exactly! You wouldn't. So, what shifts can you make today that can help you get there?

Since I've stopped drinking, I noticed I don't like when someone makes up an excuse for something and their first words are "I can't do xyz." When I hear someone say this, I tell them instead to say, "I don't want to do xyz" and see how that feels. I don't like to make excuses for something that I really don't want to do. It is okay if you don't want to do it, but by saying you can't, it takes on a life of its own.

Chapter Exercise:

Take out a piece of paper, or your journal. On one piece of paper, write out things that you have told yourself that you cannot do. No matter how big or small it is. On the next piece of paper, take each sentence that you wrote and instead of writing "I can't," write "I don't want to." As you do this, check in with yourself and see how you feel.

By checking in with yourself after each statement, you start to see how certain statements feel to you. Does it feel like the statement fits? Does it make you feel bad? In this way, you can start to see the beliefs and values that you hold about certain things in your life. Do you not want to do it? Or do you not want to put the work into doing it? Ultimately, it is your choice.

How To Get On The Right Path

Focusing on your path and what it is that you want to make of your life is a good way to start. How do we take the path to healing our complaining muscles? Ask yourself the following questions:

1. What is my goal?
2. Where do I want to be?
3. How am I going to get there?
4. What will it look like when I get there?

I listen to a lot of podcasts, interviews of people who have found their purpose, and read a lot of books about how people have changed their lives, and you know how they do it? By taking decisive action on the goals that they create.

My goal at the beginning of my journey was to stop drinking for 90 days and get up earlier in the morning. In the beginning, I did not think about what it would look like when I got there. Nor did I know what changes I was expecting to see. I wanted to have more consistency in my life, to be happier and to take charge of my life. The only steps that I knew to take was to stop drinking cold turkey and to set the alarm on my computer in my office so that once it went off, I had to get out of bed and start my day. The rest is putting action behind your plan.

When you think about where you want to be once you hit these goals, don't just think about where you physically want to be, but also mentally, emotionally and spiritually. Use all five senses to describe what you get out of hitting your goal. If your goal is to lose 30 pounds by Christmas for the Santa Sleigh Run, think about how to prepare for the weather. How will your body feel? Will you have people there with you? Create and visualize a world that is relevant to you achieving that goal so that you can immerse yourself and be present in it.

To be honest, I did not ask myself these questions. Basically, I picked a date to stop drinking, made the choice, and on that day, I started my journey. I did the work, I made mistakes, and I took note of all the important decisions I made so that I could help you start where you need to. Can you start the process without a plan? Of course you can! I did. It is not about knowing all the answers right away. It's about taking the steps, being more present in your decisions, and figuring out the bigger picture in your life. Your answers can be general, as long as you start.

The easiest way to create goals is to use the SMART goal system. SMART stands for specific, measurable, attainable, relevant and time specific. There are two things that you need to know about creating SMART goals. The first is that it is important that the path that you are tracking is the relevant path that you are creating. The second is that it is equally important to create the goals and actually take the steps. I cannot express this enough. Creating the goals and then doing nothing is not going to get you where you want to go.

About a year before I got married, my friends and I went wedding dress shopping. Although I was not sure I wanted to wear a dress, we found the perfect dress for me. I bought it and gave it to one of my bridesmaids to hold onto it.

At the time, my body weight did not fluctuate that much, so I figured if I found the dress that I wanted, it would be fine by the time my wedding came. Over the months leading to my wedding, we gathered everything we needed for decorations, did the planning, and everything was running smoothly.

My maids of honor and I set up a meeting for final looks, trying on the wedding dress and talking about final preparations about three months before the wedding. That March, I went to my friend's house, and we facetimed the other who lived in Nebraska. My friend pulled my dress out of the closet, and I started to put it on. As my friend started to zip up my dress, I could feel the tightness around my ribs and back… Oh shit! I couldn't fit in my dress!! So, you know what I did? I tried to suck it in as tight as I could, and that didn't work at all. I was so sad and distraught that my dress didn't fit. How could I not fit in it? I hadn't changed anything with my food intake. I didn't feel like I had gained weight or gotten thicker. I wasn't sure what I was going to do, and my friends wondered the same.

I sat and thought for a moment, and I told them I had three months to fit into my dress. I was determined because I didn't have the money to buy another dress. I had no idea how to lose weight or if I could even lose the weight in the places I gained it. So, I decided that I would start running a few times a week so that I could lose the inches I had gained around my stomach and back.

If I were to put this in the SMART goal system, this is what it would look like:

Specific: Fit into my size 4 wedding dress by my wedding date in June.

Measurable: I have to lose a few inches to my waist and back.

Attainable: My dress fit perfectly when I bought it, so I know that I can fit it again.

Relevant: I am getting married, and I have no other options.

Time-sensitive: I have 90 days until my wedding.

For three months, I ran. At this time, I don't remember if I changed my eating habits, but I remember that I was dedicated to running. There were a lot of things that I was not sure of. I didn't know how many inches I needed to lose around my stomach and back. I didn't know if running alone was going to help either. I stuck to the plan and I kept going. Every day, I thought about fitting back into my dress. When I didn't feel like running or when I felt like I couldn't run anymore, I kept running! I didn't have my dress to try on whenever I wanted. I had one shot. One Shot!! And for my wedding day, I was not going to miss it.

The day of my wedding was a mess of hospital visits and vertigo, but when I got to the venue an hour before the ceremony was to begin, the last thing I knew I had to deal with was whether or not my dress was going to fit. I remember going into the bathroom with my girls and getting my dress ready. I stepped into my dress for the first time in three months and as they wrapped it around my waist, stomach and back to zip it up, it fit perfectly! I worked non-stop to make sure that my dress fit on my wedding day. It took a plan, action, and grit.

A goal is just a dream until you take action. Your goal is not going to come to life all by itself. Take it one day at a time and keep going until you reach your goal.

Chapter Exercise:

We are going to adapt the exercise from earlier in this chapter to change our mindset on the negativity we feed ourselves. On one side of your paper, write out the things that you feel have not gone right in your life. This can be any aspect of your life. Once you have your list, turn that paper over, and take one of those complaints and solve it. Run through every idea in your mind that your feel would resolve the complaint completely. We're not looking for band-aid solutions, we are looking to eliminate this complaint completely. What would it take for this complaint to no longer rule your life? Once you have your list of resolutions, take it through the SMART goals system. Grab another sheet of paper and at the top put the resolution. This is now your goal. Go through the different steps: specific, measurable, attainable, relevant and time specific, and create your system. Then, do it!!

A lot of times, resolutions take trial and error. The first goal may work, but you will never know if you don't go through the steps. Take your time and give yourself grace. We are not looking for overnight success. We are looking for consistency. We are looking forward to the goal. Let's heal that part of us that wants to complain.

Reason # 6

Because This Cycle Is Familiar... And I'm Comfortable With Familiar

Accountability

I have a lot of stories about when I got so drunk I couldn't move the next morning. Or the times that I would go out, and I was able to hold my liquor better than the rest of them, even though I was often tinier than them. There were times that my ex-girlfriend and I would get plastered just because we could. It was a badge of honor really.

I know that for a long time I did not think I had a problem. What was an alcoholic? What did that look like?

At one particular therapy session, I told my therapist that I was drinking a bottle of wine every day during COVID. I thought that because I was having a rough time with quarantine and not seeing my friends, that this was normal. She breached the topic of me being an alcoholic and I shut that down immediately. The last thing that I wanted to be associated with was an alcoholic. I mean, I was functional. I didn't need to drink; I wanted to drink. I could stop anytime that I wanted. So, I couldn't be an alcoholic, right?

Then there were moments that continued to happen and it made me think that I needed to start paying more attention to my behavior.

When did I start to notice a change needed to be made?

Maybe, it was the time that I was supposed to have a Zoom date with a friend of mine and I passed out drunk and missed the call. Maybe, it was that time I got drunk at a BBQ, insisted I was fine, and drove home to my boyfriend's house. In the middle of the night, I woke up, drank some water, and threw it up. I nonchalantly went back to sleep and didn't speak of it until later that day as if it were normal. Maybe, it was all those times that I woke up hungover, wishing I hadn't drunk so much. Maybe, it was the sea of wine bottles that laid on my kitchen floor for months. Any one of these times could be when I noticed something wasn't quite right, but there was one situation that made me realize that I was making the right decision to quit drinking.

One month after I decided that I was going to stop drinking for 90 days, my ex-girlfriend and I were on the phone talking. We were drinking and I didn't realize that she was going through a tough time. She didn't really talk about it before, and she wasn't one to talk about her feelings. That night, we were talking about a lot of stuff that was going on and at one point she told me that she was excited to go see a musical.

Now, I had never expressed to her that I wanted to go to this particular musical with her or that I was even interested in seeing it, and at that moment, I instantly was envious and in my feelings. Instead of saying, "that's nice", or "that's really cool, when are you going?" I shat all over it. I was upset that she was going with someone other than me and expressed as much. It was as if I was saying to her "how dare you go to this musical without me?" I could hear her retreat on the phone. She then told me that someone else had bought the tickets for her. As she went on, she said that she didn't like that I spoke down on the experience when she was really looking forward to it and it was the one good thing that was happening in her life right now.

Now that I think about it, I think that she was trying to have a serious conversation about what was going on with her, but because she never talked to me about serious things, or she joked a lot, and we were drinking, I didn't take it seriously. She had changed the subject to put a lighter spin on the conversation and when I killed it with my negativity, it made her feel worse. We got off the phone because I knew I wasn't in the right state of mind to talk to her about it or to even apologize.

The next day, I attempted to apologize via text. I felt super shitty about how I acted the night before. I knew that it was a mix of drinking and my envy, but it did nothing to help the situation. I knew that there would be consequences for my actions and that I had hurt our relationship. It was then that I was happy that I was going to stop drinking.

I don't believe that I hit the proverbial rock bottom, but I realized that I couldn't keep going on destroying relationships in the way that I had been. I thought that I could be better without it, even though there were no clues to the contrary. The issues in my life, at my job, and in my relationships were building and I didn't know what to do or how to fix them. I needed to do something so that I felt better about the way that I acted instead of feeling shame or guilt. I knew that most of my problems weren't created by my drinking, but I knew that having a clearer head would help me figure it out.

It was at this moment that I decided to take accountability for my life, my actions, and the path that I was on. This type of accountability can take place at any point in your life. You don't have to be healing from addiction, or trauma to take accountability. Accountability is realizing that you have done something wrong, apologizing for the actions, and making sure that action doesn't happen again.

Accountability is taking responsibility for your actions, situations and the like. For most, accountability is hard. It sometimes requires people to admit that they are wrong or that they did something that was seen as unacceptable to another.

I am sure that many of you have dealt with others who do not take accountability. It may be that you also struggle with accountability. For most people, taking accountability can cause of shame. You think that you cannot do anything right in your life or that you took a misstep and it ended badly. Shame often keeps people from making a change by making them feel like everyone is judging them for their choices.

I am here to tell you that when you are on the journey to finding your new self and treating those around you differently, it will suck to take accountability for the actions that you did in the past or the mistakes that you continue to make. People who go to Alcoholics Anonymous know what it's like to feel shame. Step number nine is to make amends with the people that you hurt because you were drinking. People seek help when they realize they made a mistake or have a problem. Do not let shame keep you from growth.

What can you do when you know that you have to take responsibility for the life that you have created so far? For most, that is a hard pill to swallow. For others, they act and they take steps to make a change and make it better. Often this is where people get stuck because they feel like they have to start all the way over in their life, but most times that is not an option. This is where you have to look at the piece of your life that feels the most disrupted and change that first.

In order to begin to break that cycle, you have to take accountability for your actions, then you have to take the steps to change the behavior.

Disrupt The Cycle

The situation with my ex helped to solidify my choice in not drinking, but the biggest catalyst was my boyfriend.

As a person who practices polyamory, my ex and I both had other partners. I met my boyfriend the May before my ex and I broke up. We had different ways of hanging out. My ex and I would go out and drink and get our kicks in that way. When my boyfriend and I first met, we went to a taco place, and I ordered a drink. I asked him if he wanted one and he told me he didn't drink. After that, we would go to events and hang out. I would drink and he wouldn't. Over time, I realized that when we hung out, I stopped drinking as much. This wasn't something that he told me to do. It was something that I wanted to do. I felt that when I was with him, I didn't need to drink and that I didn't need to "hide" from him.

I felt better about who I was. I got to be loud in body, spirit, and vocally. I became more aware of myself and what I wanted. I started to see that there was a different side to me that I had forgotten and missed. I had to ask myself, why had I kept the drinking cycle?

We have to think about how the drinking cycle makes us feel and why we want to continue in that feeling. Do you feel as if drinking is the reward of displacement or security? Do you feel as if drinking is the solution to feeling better? You can ask these questions with any habit that you are trying to change. These questions help you to take accountability and then start to break away from the cycle.

Within these cycles, we realize that as the days, months, and years go by, people are dying younger and younger. We realize that the situation we complain about every other day has not changed. We have made no effort to move in a different direction, and we are stuck in the same old routine. Now, we are so comfortable where we are, that we feel that if we do move and change, it's going to be painful and hard. And sometimes it will be.

How do we get out of the same patterns and the old way of thinking?

Think about your favorite place to drive to. You love this place so much and because you have been there a lot, you have etched the directions in your brain. Every single time that you go to this place, you take the same exact route from your home. Then one day, one of the streets is closed for construction. What do you do? You may falter a bit, but you quickly find an alternative route. This is change. The construction creates an unforeseen circumstance that for a split second made us uncomfortable and change took place. For the next few weeks, or months if you live in Ohio, you take an alternate route creating a new path. You eventually go back to your original path, but now you alternate every once in a while, to keep the new route fresh.

This is a simple example of how breaking the cycle works. Instead of continuing on the same path, we get uncomfortable, take accountability, figure out the solution, fix it and make different choices.

To help keep you on track in your journey, whether it is quitting an old habit or creating a new one, you want to enlist people to help and hold you accountable. Especially if this is something that you truly want to change.

The people you enlist can be your family, best friend, or co-worker. They can even be a therapist, counselor or clergy member. This person has to be someone who motivates you and will hold you accountable when you fall back into your old ways. These are people who you can talk to about the issues that you are having, and they can help guide you through the process or talk you off the proverbial ledge. No matter who you enlist, make sure that these are people that you trust. This type of disruption ensures that you are not alone.

Then you move forward.

Put one foot in front of the other and allow yourself to grow and move through the shame and disappointment, process the emotions that come up, and then let it go.

In the movie 8 Mile, Eminem's character, Rabbit, went to the final battle prepared. Rabbit was spiraling about the things Papa Doc could have used against him and he decided to do something daring. Instead of giving him the chance, Rabbit used Papa Doc's ammo in his favor. He began the rap battle by talking about his flaws and how messed up his life is. He took the power away from Papa Doc. He no longer had anything to say that would destroy his competition. That is how we break the cycle. We are putting the power back in our own hands. Stop fighting for your life and be as authentic and real as you can. You messed up. Own it. You made decisions that hurt others. Own it! Now, change it. Show up differently to those who continue to stay in your life and prove to yourself that you are more than the past you.

After many years of not wanting to go to therapy because I thought that it did not work, I started seeing a therapist after my ex-husband left. I was so angry in my daily life, and I could not understand why. I was working full-time, I felt as if I couldn't make ends meet, and I was lashing out at my closest friends and partners. I didn't know what I was going to do and I certainly didn't know how I was going to manage my life now that he was gone. It felt like I was falling into a black hole, and I didn't know what to do about it. I wasn't that comfortable with myself, and I also did not have the stability that I thought. I didn't know what comfort and stability looked or felt like. I didn't know what comfortability was without a person. Although I had my friends, I needed to find other ways to dump all of the pent-up emotions I felt from my situation, so I decided that I would start going to therapy. I needed to talk to someone about what was going on in my life and how I could find solutions to any problems that I was dealing with.

I chose a random therapist within my network and when I walked into her office, I got started by telling her everything that I could in that first meeting. I wanted to be clear about why I was there, what I wanted to accomplish in therapy and how this was going to help me move forward. After the session, she gave me a booklet to fill out that would help her get to know me more, my goals and how she could support me.

Over the next few months, things started to become clear. I realized that my anger came from shouldering the blame of everything that went wrong in my marriage, instead of only taking accountability for the things that I was responsible for. I held the weight of the actions that he took and made them my own. I put a lot of undue pressure on myself to be better in areas that he failed at, instead of working on my own downfalls. Over time, I started to let go of the parts of our relationship that I was not responsible for. I became less angry and I was able to feel more at peace with myself and start the process of forgiving myself.

As I stated in the beginning of this book, I did not realize that this was going to be a lonely journey. I did not always feel that people understood what I was going through. Most didn't know why I decided to do it at the time that I did. I wasn't talking to the same people that I did when I was drinking, and I didn't really see how they were going to help me. Even when I went out with them, I felt so out of place. You will feel out of place for a bit until you find your tribe, the group of people who are doing exactly what you are doing or who support you on your journey. You begin to see that you have people who know what you are going through.

Like most people, I had preconceived notions about what therapy meant. My experience with counseling and therapy has been on and off since I was a kid. After I was molested, I ended up going to counseling. For many years after those sessions, I felt that counseling did not work for me. We were limited in the subjects that we talked about, and I still had triggers around my experience.

When my ex-husband left, I found solace in talk therapy. It was one of the first things that I did to do a sanity check. I wanted someone who was an unbiased party to guide me through the emotions I was feeling. I was very angry, in a new relationship and I knew that things were not going to end well because of my attitude. I saw my therapist for about nine months or so until she retired. During this time, I was able to talk to an unbiased party about my thoughts, feelings and emotions and anything that I needed clarity on or help with. I was thinking about how I wanted to show up and what I could change in order to make things better in my life, and she was able to guide me.

When my therapist retired, I felt like I was in a better place and my attitude had gotten better. I was getting my first book ready for publishing, and I hosted a 14-day Online Summit for trauma-informed coaches. The summit went well, but after 16 weeks of work, I was burnt out. I ended up looking for a new therapist a few months after that.

We are hearing more about talk therapy as an option to help us through any situations or feelings that we are not able to process on our own. I hear a lot of advertisements on social media and on podcasts where I did not hear many before. We are looking for a way to connect and to understand ourselves to be better people, and it is good that people are looking for therapy to do it. I believe that the pandemic made some of us look at ourselves and our lives and made us want to change. People have gone through a lot in their lives and have experienced many different traumas, and the pandemic was the straw that broke the camel's back for most millennials. People are hurting, they want to feel more connected in this chaotic world of ours, they want to break the cycle and the chains that hold them back, and they want to find ways to get the help they need in their situations.

Releasing Unwanted Energy

The funny thing about life is that we see the things that bother us and often do nothing about it. We hold onto a lot of emotions. We take everything said personally. We let our anger out on others. Have you ever thought about why you do the things that you do? Why do you hold onto the familiar? What are the patterns that you see in your life that keep you coming back?

For me, I repeatedly got into the same types of relationships. I noticed that I felt trapped just as I did when I was a kid, and instead of taking myself away from it, I decided that I could probably endure it a little bit longer. We tell ourselves it's about building resilience. We tell others that what doesn't kill us makes us stronger. We stay in survival mode and wear it like a badge of honor. What is it that makes us say, "Yes, I will take another shot" when we know that the next one is going to make us black out?

When you have been in survival mode for so long, it is easier to take your hands off the wheel and let someone else do the driving, even if that person is not the greatest thing for you. I talk about this in my very first podcast episode called "A Learned Silence/A Learned Suffering" which is available to listen to on YouTube.

In many ways, we are taught that shame and suffering are a part of life. In order to get more, you have to suffer. My ex-husband thought that way. He would say that we have to suffer in order to get what we want. That is what I thought when I was a kid. That is what I thought when I was drinking. I can do this again and again. The suffering makes me resilient and strong. In reality, I was creating a cage that allowed life to happen to me.

We don't realize that we are holding onto energy that no longer serves us. We don't want the energy of being strong anymore. Why do you think people are telling us to check on our strong friends? We don't want to take another beating in life because we feel that we have to. We want to let it go so that we can move on, get ourselves out of survival mode, and create a life that we can thrive in. Survival is no longer the goal. We want to finally shed this unwanted energy. One of the ways to do this is by journaling.

Journaling is a way for you to vent out all of your frustrations with words that you may want to say to others but know that it may be best for you not to. For almost a year straight, I journaled through my non-drinking journey. It felt so good to get a lot of things off my brain and onto paper so that I didn't have to hold it any longer. Sometimes our emotions get so heavy that we just want to put them down. We wonder if it is the right time to tell the person or if we want to get it out and then burn it. This is a good start to formulating those thoughts and having the energetic release of pen to paper.

When I brought up journaling to vent to a friend of mine, they told me that journaling is cool and helps you to get your thoughts out, but sometimes it is good to use your voice and say the things that you are thinking. In some ways I think they are right.

To participate in this method, you will need two chairs. Place the chairs facing each other. Sit in one of the chairs facing the empty chair. Imagine the person that you want to talk to is sitting in that empty chair. You can do this with your eyes open or closed. After you have them held in your mind, vocalize all the things that you want to say to this person with no repercussions. You can yell, scream, curse, or whatever feels good to you in the moment. This is a form of energy release. It may sound very silly, but it works. Take a moment and try it. Think about a situation that you have not fully resolved with someone. It could be because you don't talk to that person any longer or maybe they no longer are with you. Set a timer for five minutes and release. You may be surprised at what comes of it.

When I went through my second round of chakra alignments, I decided that this would be the best exercise for me to do after meditating on my throat chakra. I had been holding on to a lot of conversations that I should have had with people in my life, but I didn't. I had written them down in my journal and told myself that I was going to talk to them about it, but I could not find the right time, or I thought that maybe it wasn't worth bringing up. Instead, I decided to record what I wanted to say to them. I recorded three different audios, one for three different people, and I let it all go. I did not send these recordings to them. They were meant to help me get the thoughts and emotions off my chest. Afterwards, it felt good. One of the recordings I did actually end up sending. I kept the others for a while and then eventually deleted them.

While seeing my new therapist, I decided to try Neuro-Emotional Technique therapy or NET. I had never heard of it and came across this form of therapy two different times. The first time I heard about it was in my developmental group.

My friend's step-grandmother is a medium and while I was doing her Pure Romance party, she invited me to stay for the readings afterwards. During the reading, I talked about a jarring spiritual experience that I had and how I wanted to learn to protect myself. She told me that the development group was a way to do so as they practiced mediumship, special gifts and other spiritual practices. I went to this group twice a month for a while and met a woman who talked about her NET session. I thought that it was kind of cool, looked it up and then kind of forgot about it.

Then, I saw it on one of my favorite primetime television shows, Grey's Anatomy. Owen, who is an army vet, was having some issues and triggers, and decided to try NET which helped him move past some of the old trauma that he experienced. That was the moment I thought, "I am going to have to try this". I waited a few more months and then I finally booked an appointment. At the time that I am writing this, I have been seeing my NET therapist for over a year. I love the work that she does and the progress that I have made.

At my first meeting, I talked to the therapist and as she explained it, I noticed that it was quite similar to Reiki except it was physical and not energetic. I understood right away that we were going to get into the sessions and release emotions. I get the most insight from these sessions as I process emotions from previous experiences that still have impact on my everyday life. It has also helped me to understand where my emotional triggers derive from which has been important on my healing journey. It is a unique process, and I am always amazed at the things that come up. Your body knows what you need, and muscle testing helps you to find what you are telling yourself verses what you know is true.

Another way to release emotions, provide understanding about your challenges, and connect with people who are also going through similar journeys, is yoga.

Yoga is a practice of listening to your body as you move and breathe through movement. You hold a pose for as long as you can, you stretch a pose out as far as your body will take you, and you get to connect with your body. Yoga has been used as a form of physical therapy for people who have trouble with their legs, body aches, weight loss, traumatic experiences, you name it! Yoga is very versatile.

Gerry first started yoga right after college. She had experienced some physical trauma in her life and was interested in what yoga could offer her as she focused on gaining back control. She signed up for a class that was in her area, and she was nervous about attending. She was not someone who regularly did workout classes, but she had heard positive feedback about yoga and was willing to give it a try.

In the first two classes, she did not really notice any difference. She attended the classes and performed the motions, but she did not quite understand what she was really doing. She focused on her breath and wondered if she looked stupid because she had never done a class before. She felt like she was just stretching her body, and nothing more. She did not know what to expect from the experience, but she kept with it. The third class she attended changed everything.

Gerry went through the poses, stretching, and breathwork, and as she did, she started to notice how her body felt. She noticed how her lungs expanded and deflated as she took in air. She noticed how her feet, legs, arms, torso, and head felt as she moved into a different position. As she held the warrior pose, her eyes welled up with tears and she began to cry. At first, it startled her. She didn't feel like she had to cry or that she was sad about anything, but the tears continued to slowly fall down her cheeks. When she reflected on the experience, she described it as a "necessary energy release." As she continued the class, she continued to cry through another pose and afterwards she felt like a weight had been lifted. When the stagnant energy in your body starts to move and release, it may come out in the form of tears, laughter, or yawns. These energy releases help to unblock parts of your body that are holding energy that is no longer needed. Sometimes emotions become loose in your everyday activities like yoga, taking a walk, or while sitting at your desk working.

It is always important that if you feel that you are not able to do something by yourself, that you enlist the help of a professional. When you know what can help you cope in a healthier way or express yourself without fear of being judged, you gain a better understanding of what you need in your life.

My NET therapist, Lindsey, told me that when she needs to release energy she will go to a park, lake, or some form of nature, and release that energy as a food source to nature. She said that when she goes out in nature, she will visualize a putrid green mist rising in her body. That mist represents the emotions that she is feeling that she is intending to release. As the mist builds and she feels the energy, she will scream or exhale all the mist. During this release, she imagines that the mist is transmuted from all the negative energy that she felt, into positive food for the plants and animals around her. The grass, trees, fish, and other wildlife eating those plants are absorbing the energy and making use of it. This may not be the method for you, as I know that a lot of people are not going out to the lake to scream at it, but who knows.

There are so many ways that you can release unwanted energy in your life. These are ones that have helped people through times in their lives that they would not have otherwise tried.

Chapter Exercise:

Choose an activity from above or create your own activity that will allow you to disrupt your old patterns and release unwanted energy. This could be signing up for a yoga class, finding a Reiki Practitioner, or going out in nature.

Journal about your experience and reflect on what energy you feel that you need to release, what energy was released during that activity, and how you plan to release energy going forward. Not only does this allow you to see what changes occur in your life, but it also helps you find what methods work for you and what methods don't.

Happy releasing.

Reason #7

Because My Triggers Control Me, And I Don't Know How To Stop Them

When You Stop Reacting And Start Studying

Now, we are going to explore our triggers and how we can stop them from controlling our lives. In my world, my triggers were the exact reason I kept drinking for as long as I did. It wasn't until months into my journey that I even realized that my triggers were part of the reason I was drinking more and more.

A trigger is a situation that brings up emotions within you from past experiences. These emotions are not usually associated with the current situation, but how a similar situation makes us feel. A trigger is the symptom of a deeper problem. Oftentimes, we do not know why something triggers us or where the trigger started, but we can begin our trigger exploration by becoming a scientist.

Becoming a scientist is a method created to understand how something works. It can be used in many different situations. After hearing this motto in 2021, Charlie used it with their business to break down what was working, what wasn't working and why they thought it wasn't working. If they were struggling with creating a web page for their authors or picking the colors for their brand, the coach would break it down by asking questions to get to the root of the problem. What was causing them to stall on their progress? How could they get back into the swing of things? There would be a different answer every time, and oftentimes the verdict came back to their emotions regarding the specific task they were doing or avoiding. Then they would create a plan to get over that hump and move forward. You cannot make progress if you are stuck.

In this case, we are not building a business. We are making changes in our life that can have a lasting positive effect. You may be struggling to decide what habit you want to change, or you may be wondering how starting a new habit will change your life. You may realize that you have a lot of habits that you want to change. You may think that starting a new habit is going to affect you in a negative way. You may decide that changing things in your life is too hard. These are all normal responses. In the end, you have to think about what the end goal is that you have in mind and create the steps to start it. Within that, you have to understand why you may be emotionally driven to continue the unhealthy habit.

Think Like a Scientist

In this activity, we are going to pull apart the habit that you want to change and discover the triggers behind that habit.

After two days of not drinking, I was triggered by something in my life, and the first thing that I wanted to do was drink. Insert facepalm. When I went through my breakup in March, I wanted to drink. I called up my best friend, sobbing, and I asked her if I could take shots. Her first response was, "Te', you're not drinking." I asked again through tears, knowing that I was not going to drink. I told her that I wanted to drink and that I wanted the pain to go away. I just wanted to drink. I didn't have liquor in the house, although I had this beautiful bottle of wine, but I did not drink.

Over the years, I learned to use alcohol to cope. It helped to numb the hurt and the pain. I didn't have to think about a solution to the problem because I was going to get back to it later. Life was too hard, so I would just drink it away now. The reality was, I never got back to it.

A year or so into my marriage, I started to notice that to have sex with my ex-husband I would self-medicate with liquor. I didn't notice it right away. It took time. I didn't realize that I was no longer attracted to him. Some of the situations that he put me through, I laugh at now with my friends, but those small put downs, or ways that he would talk about me to others was the start of being unattracted to who he was as a person. When I wanted sex, I would drink or smoke marijuana to get things moving. It helped for a while. Then when things really took a turn, we stopped sleeping in the same bed altogether and I was no longer interested in sharing my body with someone who seemed not to care about my well-being. When we were no longer together, I was talking with a woman about this, and she said that she used to do the same thing. In that moment, I realized that that was not uncommon and of course I learned later that we were dealing with our situation the best way that we knew how at the time. We could have talked to our spouse about it, or we could have stopped having sex with our spouses until we figured out a solution, but we chose to cover it up instead.

When we look at the triggers of the previous examples, I cannot use the general breakup of my partner or not being attracted to my ex-husband as a trigger. This assumes that that every breakup I go through or every time my partner made me feel unattractive, I would have a reason to drink. It is not that simple. I have had many breakups in my life, and I did not drink after they happened. You must look deeper than the surface issue. The breakup is just a symptom, not the trigger.

When I drank, it felt like my world was literally falling apart. Think *Chicken Little* and "the sky is falling." Yea, like that. I knew that I felt pain like this before, and this time it felt unbearable. What was I going to do? How was I going to move forward? Would I ever get into a relationship again? I went into doom and gloom mode.

Then I became a scientist. I had to know what the trigger was and how to get to the root of it. So, I journaled every day to see if there were any patterns of triggering, or if I could find the underlying emotion to it all. Now was the time to discover myself at the core. The emotions that came up for me after that breakup were sadness, guilt, shame, anger, disappointment, embarrassment, disrespect, insignificant, betrayed, violated, and taken for granted. These are not emotions that I have often, and I rarely sit with them to figure out why they are.

Your triggers can be correlated to past traumas, situational traumas, or a learned behavior due to a specific situation or things you saw in your life. The goal is to find the trigger, process it, and let it go so that it hurts less and triggers you less when it happens. When do you get angry, sad, depressed, or excited? Does something trigger this emotion? What is it? In order to control how situations trigger you, you have to understand the underlying reason that the trigger exists.

All of our lives, we create coping mechanisms to help us deal with the situations that we have been through. They help us walk away, go into ourselves, or even avoid the horrors that were once our lives, and we keep using them thinking that they are what is keeping us safe now. My coping mechanism at the time was I would push down the emotions and numb the pain. There was nothing a bottle of wine couldn't fix.

Now, look back at the impact of the coping mechanisms that you created in your life, your relationships, and your mood. What is it that helps you? What emotion does it elicit and how does it help? Like someone who smokes cigarettes, it is used to help sooth and calm them in times of stress.

For others, their coping mechanism can be a sense of safety. For me, it was a way to escape and not think about what I had to do or what needed to be done. Are these coping mechanisms helping you or hindering you?

In my situation, drinking was hindering me from understanding my emotions and dealing with the situations head on. I was not talking about my problems, feelings or creating solutions that would better my situation. I believe if I drank when I broke up with my partner, I would have cried, had my emotional breakdown, and things could have gotten much darker and there is a possibility that I would still be stuck in those emotions after a year. Instead, I looked back at my relationship and saw the good, and the bad. I could understand why that relationship no longer served me, my situation, and the person that I was becoming. It took me two months to get out of my soul death, but once I did, I was able to see that I was better off.

For a year, I avoided places that she would be in more often than I can count. I saw her three times after our breakup, and each time I was given more clarity on why it ended. At this point in my journey, I hold no resentment towards her, or the situation. I gave too much to someone who was not giving as much to me. I know that it would have taken me much longer to figure that out if I had continued to drink. I know this, the things that I saw were not different from when we had first started dating after a year. I stayed because I thought it would change after we talked. I thought I could do more, and it would help. Drinking kept my brain foggy, and it helped me to become subdued to my situation. I finally had enough of being angry and the stagnation that I felt in my relationship.

Explore the things that trigger you and pair them with the coping mechanisms you are using to cover up emotions and get rid of them. That is not a way to live. You will see what situations and emotions make you turn to that unhealthy habit and how you can change your mind to a healthier choice. I realized that there were things that triggered my drinking, not that it was just a habit. Understanding your triggers is a huge part of knowing why a habit has formed in the first place. I knew that stress or high-tension situations made me want to drink. I also knew that having a drink would calm my nerves before the tension arrived, so I would drink. When it came to the TV, I had to break the trigger of making dinner and walking into the den. Once I understood that trigger, I could slowly start integrating into watching TV again. Know your triggers.

Creating New Coping Mechanisms

As you go on the journey of changing your habits, the one thing that you will notice is the need for new coping mechanisms. Coping mechanisms are the unconscious or conscious thoughts and behaviors people use to manage stressful situations and uncomfortable emotions. Everyone has a coping mechanism that they use to help regulate and not all coping mechanisms are unhealthy.

Creating new coping mechanisms can be just as difficult as creating a new habit. You are looking for a way to help reduce stress in your life that you managed in one way for many years. When you start to explore your coping mechanisms, be a scientist and try any method that you believe would work best for you. To help new coping mechanisms stick, you want to choose one to change. When you try to change all of your unhealthy coping mechanisms at once, you can halt your progress altogether. Think about people who want to exercise more at the beginning of the year, and they try to do everything all at once. By the time they hit the end of January, they are ready to quit or have already. The goal is to make a healthier choice to combat stress, so we want to start with one unhealthy coping mechanism to get rid of.

We should start by figuring out our coping mechanisms. Do you know what they are? How did you learn these coping mechanisms? Were they self-taught or did you pick them up from someone else? Take a moment to ask yourself, what are the treatments that you use in high, emotional situations? What do you do to sooth yourself? They have probably helped you through many changing phases of your life. Then ask yourself, is this coping mechanism that I use considered healthy or unhealthy?

I know a number of people who smoke cigarettes. Some smoke only when they drink, others smoke when they are stressed, and some smoke because they still think it's cool. When I was a kid, I felt like I saw my mom smoke a lot. I remember when we went to the gas station, she would pump her gas, dig into her coin ashtray, go inside and get a pack of cigarettes. You know, when you could do that. After my mom quit smoking, I asked her why she would start back up again. She said that when life got a bit too stressful, she would smoke because it helped to calm her. Eventually, she broke the cycle and stopped smoking altogether. I believe my mom stopped smoking cold turkey, but not everyone can do that.

I was invited to a birthday party with a group of friends who at that time I had not seen since the summer before I stopped drinking. When I got to the party, I got comfortable and started to catch up with everyone and the new things that were going on in their lives. After some karaoke, I went into the kitchen to grab a snack, and I looked over at my friend Shirley. We started talking and I caught a glimpse of a silver whistle around her neck. My first thought was "what in the world is that?" So, I asked her. And when she answered, I thought it was genius!

Shirley said that it was to help her stop smoking cigarettes and vapes, and it was working. When she feels the need to smoke, she puts the whistle to her mouth, and sucks in as if taking a hit of a cigarette. The whistle is silent, so it didn't bother others in her vicinity. Most of the time, you see people who want to quit cigarette smoking using a vape to get the nicotine that they crave. She had tried to stop smoking with vapes but found that her whistle was better. She found a way to still perform the action of smoking without the harmful chemicals. This coping mechanism was a great replacement for her because it essentially mocked the action without having to light up.

Sometimes your coping mechanisms are about the substance that you are putting into your body. Oftentimes, it's linked to the action itself. As you learn the difference, your coping mechanisms will be actions that you take to relax before dealing with the problem at hand. This is why it is so important to learn your triggers before getting to this step.

To figure out the new coping mechanisms that you would like to create, first let's figure out what coping mechanisms you use already. Take out a pen and piece of paper or a journal and write down what methods you use when you get stressed, mad, or sad. These coping mechanisms may look like substance abuse, isolation, overeating, alcohol, aggression, and impulsive spending, just to name a few. I have included a chart for you to see what other unhealthy coping mechanisms you may have.

When I was seeing my therapist after my ex-husband left, I went to a session and talked to her about all the things that I had done the night before. I mentioned that I had drunk a bottle of wine, which is the equivalent of four glasses of wine. My therapist mentioned that she was concerned about my drinking because it seemed excessive. I told her that I did it more often since COVID, but I did not think that I had a problem. After that, I stopped talking to her about it. What I did not realize was that drinking was a form of escape and denial and I was using it as an excuse to not deal with the underlying issues. My therapist was rightfully concerned, and I felt that that was not a problem that needed to be fixed at that time. Eventually, I followed the patterns of my drinking, my moods, and my relationships and found that it was a coping mechanism.

Once you have written down the unhealthy coping mechanisms that you use, now it's time to figure out which one we are going to change first.

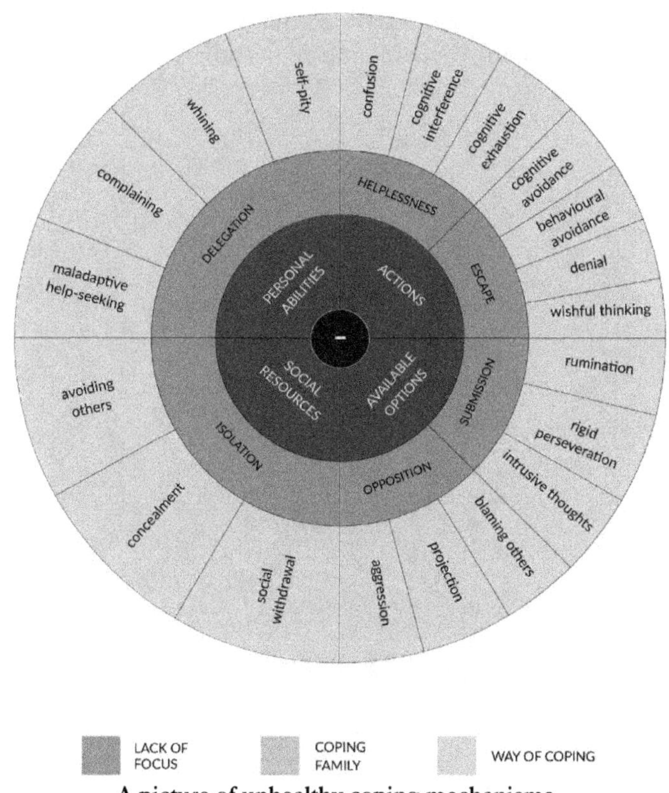

A picture of unhealthy coping mechanisms.
https://positivepsychology.com/unhealthy-coping-mechanisms/

On my journey, I found a few new coping mechanisms that work. When I get stressed, overwhelmed or anxious about life, I cannot think or sit to meditate. I begin to feel restless and because I am not able to do anything, I stop everything! So, I decided to find ways that helped me to get rid of the stagnant energy fast which started as running. Now I know what some of you may be thinking… I am not running anywhere! Or I don't run unless I'm being chased. I completely understand that. There are other ways to physically get rid of that energy. You can take a walk, go to the park and play, go bowling, paint, or even go to a rage room. When I am in a space to slow down, I will meditate, put together a puzzle or Lego set. During that time, I am able to reflect, think about the situation and come up with resolutions if needed. Once you have found a few coping mechanisms that work for you, start right away. The next time something happens that causes you stress, overwhelm or sadness, replace your old coping mechanism with the new one. Find one that fits you best. I have included a graph of healthy coping mechanisms that can help you with your list.

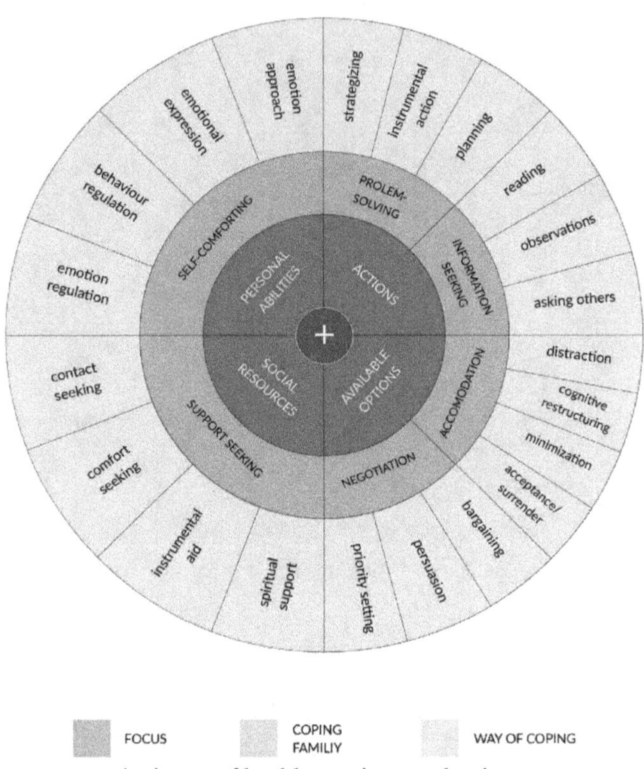

A picture of healthy coping mechanisms.
https://positivepsychology.com/unhealthy-coping-mechanisms/

When I started to notice my triggers and the actions I took when I became stressed, I noticed that I would have the urge to pour myself a drink. I never associated the behavior of pouring myself a drink as a way to prepare for the buzz that would help me forget that I had a problem to deal with. It took me a couple of months to realize that I received a calming effect from pouring myself a glass of wine or an alcoholic beverage knowing that after I downed the drink I would get lit. The behavior of pouring a drink was needed, just as much as waiting for the buzz to kick in. Think about my friend with the metal tube for smoking. Sometimes the behavior is calming. Now that I have stopped drinking for a year and a half, I still get pleasure from pouring myself a drink when I am stressed. It is a signal that something is bothering me and that I should focus on my emotions.

The key to sticking with the new coping mechanisms is consistency. When I stopped drinking, I was talking to someone about my journey. They told me that they had decided to stop drinking for two months. When I asked them how it was going, they did not respond as I had thought they would. I knew from what I had experienced, I was happy with the energy that I gained, the mood changes, and I had started to see the changes in my skin. Their response, "Being sober is boring." They told me that they did it to take a break from drinking for a little bit, but they didn't like it at all. They liked the feeling of being drunk and they felt that any activity they did while they were sober was not the same as when they were drunk. I knew that they were going to go back to drinking as soon as their time was up.

The reasons that people make changes in their life and stick with them are going to be different for everyone. I kept going after 90 days because I realized that I didn't want to wake up in the morning with a hangover. I didn't want to go back to having a fucked-up attitude about life and avoiding my problems because it may inconvenience someone else. I was tired of not being happy or living my best life because I was too busy worried about how others would feel about me.

What are the reasons that you are changing your coping mechanisms? How have they kept you from making decisions in your life or dealing with a problem that kept manifesting? How much longer do you want to deal with the backlash of not controlling your life? Yes, discipline can be boring. Yes, not drinking can be boring. Yes, not a lot of people like routine. Your motivation to create a happier and healthier environment will help you to stay consistent. Your persistence will help you see the results of your actions.

As you move through your healing journey, your coping mechanisms will help you calm your mind and understand a situation before you take action.

Chapter Exercise:

For one week, find a new hobby or activity to do that will help you relieve stress and make you happy when you feel triggered. We are told that we have to be a functioning member of society where most of us are unhappy. Most of us don't know ourselves because we play too many roles in our lives. What they don't tell you is that within those roles, you still have to find time to nurture yourself, find what you like to do without anyone else around, and do things that will make you happy as well. This does not have to be a bath or getting a mani-pedi. It could be taking a walk in the park, going axe throwing, or writing in your journal. It could be sitting down and reading that new book that you bought.

During the week, schedule 30 minutes to yourself. On the weekend, schedule an hour or two for yourself. As you go forward, schedule 30-60 minutes a week for you to give back to yourself and find what brings you pleasure. When you are happy, it shows in everything that you do. Stop only living to take care of others. Live for your happiness.

From Observation To Evidence

If you have read this book from the beginning, you know what habits you are going to break. You know what new habits you want to form. You know why you want to make changes in your life, and you know the triggers that play a part in them. So, what's next? Now you have to track your progress.

Just like any goal that you want to achieve, you must have a way to track the progress that you are making. This will help you see how the habit affected you in your life, relationship, and career, and how your life has changed without it.

Our lives are bombarded with different tracking systems. Some are simple and easy to follow. Others are a bit more detailed in their approach. It really depends on what you are tracking. Are you tracking your food intake and calories? Or are you tracking how many days you have stopped smoking and your cravings? For those who are tech savvy, there are plenty of apps out there that will help you track how many days you have gone without a cigarette or a drink. There are also apps out there that will track the exact foods that you eat, the amount that you eat, and it will calculate how many calories you have ingested during the day. For some of the old school folks, a pen and paper or a paper calendar works fine as well.

When I stopped drinking, I did not mark off a calendar. I started on January 2 and I counted out 90 days to know the exact day I would hit my goal. I tracked my day-to-day progress, thoughts, and triggers by journaling. I wrote about how I felt and what changes I could see.

In the beginning, the one change I noticed is that I stopped reaching for a bottle and started reaching for the sparkling water. I wrote about wanting to drink, some of the triggers that caused me to crave alcohol and explored the emotions I was feeling. I realized that my need to drink was to escape the emotions or stress that was going on at that moment, and every day that I didn't drink, I wrote it down in my journal.

As you begin to make changes in your life, seeing exactly what you have accomplished on your journey is a great motivator to keep going. Before this book even began, I summarized my journey and year of transformation. I went through each month of 2023 and gave you a snapshot of what changed, how I felt, and things I did to overcome the hurdles of not having the drinking "safety net".   There were so many small changes that snowballed into big changes, and I could not even begin to tell you how good it feels. As you continue your path of healing and transforming, keep an eye on the changes.

To become better at tracking your goals and how well you are doing with your habits, you must become better at creating your goals or new habits. What is it that you want to accomplish? Your goals should be specific, measurable, achievable, relevant, and time bound. Creating S.M.A.R.T. goals are a way to help you not only track your progress, but they also help you stay on track with them.

In this book, you have chosen what habit you want to change and why. That helps with the specific part of goal setting. Here, we explore a bit more about the habit. For example, I will have no alcoholic beverages for 90 days. Answer the questions: who, what, when, where, and why. These questions will help you flush out the specifics of the habit you want to change.

Then you must decide how you are going to measure your progress. I kept track of my non-drinking through journaling. You can use planners, calendars, and habit or goal trackers. Pick a tracker that works best for you and one that you will stick with. When you are creating your tracker, you want to make sure that you know what you are tracking. For me, I was tracking my mood, my triggers, and noting the days I did not drink. Pick metrics that are right for you on your journey and will help you stay focused.

The next step is to understand if the goal is achievable. This means the goal is realistic and within reach, but challenging. Cutting alcohol from my system for 90 days is achievable, yet I knew it was going to be tough. You also want to ask yourself; do you have the necessary skills and resources to accomplish this goal? I was in therapy at the time that I decided to quit drinking, and I knew that taking alcohol out of my home and stopping my wine membership were necessary steps. Most goals are achievable as long as you are setting a realistic expectation. Most people will not go from working out zero days a week to five days a week and be able to sustain that type of activity for a long period of time. Take your time and explore what changing your specific habit will look like.

Now we can explore how this habit is relevant to your life and your long-term goals. At first, I wanted to stop drinking because a meme told me to and challenged my thinking on why I needed alcohol. This meme was not relevant to me. It was the idea that not drinking could help me understand my emotions, I would be able to think more clearly, and I wouldn't have to wake up to a hangover. I was going through a tough time in my life, and I wanted to feel better physically, emotionally and mentally, and I didn't think I could do that if I continued drinking and avoiding the problems that I had in my life. What will changing this habit do for you and your life? How will you feel?

The last thing that you want to do is make the goal time bound. What is the timeframe that you want to accomplish this change? Do you want to do this in 90 days, or do you want to give yourself six months? It is your choice. I told myself that I was only going to stop drinking for 90 days to see what would happen. That would put my ending timeframe at the beginning of April. By the time I got to April, I decided to continue on the journey. I wanted to finish my chakra alignment sober since I had never done that before. It would push my timeframe to mid-May, but I was seeing the changes and knew that pushing a bit more couldn't hurt. When mid-May rolled around, I realized it was almost the middle of the year, and I adjusted my goal to the end of 2023. I was motivated to continue. Decide how long you want to try this habit. In Chapter 1, I note that it takes, on average, 66 days to form a new habit. I would suggest starting there and going for more if you wish.

To showcase how this works with another habit, let's use the example of changing your eating habits. If you were to start this as your habit, maybe you would first purchase a weekly dry erase board and place it on your fridge. By having it in the kitchen, you will see it every day and it is conveniently located next to the food. At the top of the dry erase board, write out the specific habit that you want to accomplish. The new habit is that you want to drink one smoothie a day and add six servings of fruits and vegetables to your diet.

Then, let's decide what metrics you want to measure and keep track of them. In each smoothie, there will be a list of three or more fruits and vegetables. While you're tracking your smoothie intake, create a food and progress journal. You can write about when your cravings for sweets, and how your co-workers bought donuts, and you decided to grab celery sticks with peanut butter instead. Write about how hard it was, and that you stuck to it and reiterate your why. You see where we're going here? A journal can help track other things associated with eating better, like weight loss, measurements, calorie intake and other things that we would like to keep track of.

Then, look at whether this habit is achievable. What measures can you take to ensure that you stick with the new habit? This is where knowing your triggers are important and what types of situations would make you want to jump into the salty and sugary treats that you crave.

Then it's time to explore how this habit is relevant to your life and what you want. In this example, eating better would make you feel healthier, less dense, and help maintain your weight. It is about making better food choices.

Finally, how long do you want to keep this up? Do you want to do this for the next 30 days? 90 days? Do you want to integrate healthier eating into your lifestyle or only for a short time? Do you want to do this gradually by not taking away all the snacks, but limiting them? How can you start to feel better about your choices and consciously decide on what snacks you'll eat while on this journey? You get to decide what you want this habit to look like in your life.

Tracking your progress takes consistency. This will be a habit that you want to practice every day and use it as much as possible. As you go through your day, you will see that method and be reminded to do the task associated with your habit. The more you track your changes in your journal or habit tracker, and see your results physically, emotionally and mentally, you will want to do more. This goes for any habit that you choose. I stated before that I did not see a change in myself until after two months of not drinking. The first changes that I noticed were mental and emotional. Eventually, I did see the physical changes, although that was not the purpose of my challenge.

Now that we have talked about tracking your habits and results, I think we should talk a bit about rewarding ourselves for our achievements. When I stopped drinking, my boyfriend wanted to encourage me to hit my goal, so he created a reward system for every 30 days that I hit my goal. He wanted to help keep me motivated, which I have to admit I didn't think about at the time. Within that, he also created consequences for if I did drink. Each of the consequences got worse as time went on, and the rewards became more desirable as I hit each milestone. I encourage you to have at least one reward in place for yourself. You are about to do some hard work, and you are going to want to congratulate yourself as you move forward. Sometimes we don't think about celebrating ourselves or giving ourselves our flowers. Celebrations are the motivation you didn't know that you needed.

When you come up with your rewards, you want to set some ground rules. For example, if you have decided that you are adding more healthy foods to your diet, then your reward should not be a trip to McDonald's after one week of eating healthily. You may decide that since you made smoothies all week that you would treat yourself to the new smoothie place instead of making a smoothie, or that you may treat yourself to a manicure.

In my case, if I achieved my 90-day goal, my boyfriend would take me to my favorite restaurant, The Melting Pot.

To stay on top of your progress, set up checkpoints to make your change worthwhile. My boyfriend thought that it would be good for me to have a checkpoint every 30 days to celebrate my accomplishment. He told me what the consequences were, but he did not tell me what the rewards were. We made sure that the consequences he came up with did not go against my boundaries but that they were undesirable if I did decide to take a sip. Over the 90-day span, the consequences got more severe. With each reward being more desirable than the previous, I was happy to work towards something, even when I didn't know what they were.

Set a timeframe for what you want to do and for every checkpoint you reach, you get a reward. Set manageable goals, achieve them, and celebrate immediately. Make the reward something that you do not do for yourself everyday so that you will be enticed to complete the checkpoint.

Chapter celebrations:

Part of your healing journey is knowing that you have to celebrate your wins. Celebrate as often as you need and with every single accomplishment that you achieve.

I met a woman named Allie and we quickly became friends because of our positive attitude and the straightforward way we deal with life. During a group call that she put together, she taught me the Trinity. This is a form of celebration where you talk about three things: you brag about an accomplishment, you share gratitude for something in your life and express your desire. I started to use this method at the end of my podcast because I felt that it was important for people to celebrate themselves as they go through life. We never received a playbook on how life is supposed to be done, but we continue to live. We make mistakes and we pick ourselves back up again.

By bragging about your accomplishments, you remind yourself that you have done great things. It can be waking up early and working out. Or it can be graduating college with your second master's degree. No matter what it is, brag about it!

Sharing what you are grateful for reminds you that you have something to be happy about in your life. I use gratitude as a pick me up when I need a boost of sunshine in my life.

Your desires are your dreams and goals that have yet to transform. Just like a child, you want to use your imagination to dream and manifest the things that you want in life. Those desires are ready to come true; you just have to believe it.

From now on, at the end of the week, write down your Trinity. Put it in a journal or put it as a note in your phone where you can see it every day. Set a calendar event in your phone for once a month, and label it "Read Trinity." Take time to go back over your journal or notes and read your Trinity. Then do it all over again.

Reason #8

Because Sobriety Means I Have To Listen To Myself... And That Terrifies Me

Do You Know What You Truly Want In Your Life?

After my breakup, I sat in Lindsey's office not knowing what I wanted or needed in my life. I felt like I fell into the same relationship pattern as I always had. I was stuck in a job that I was ready to leave. I knew what I wanted to pursue, and I wasn't sure how to get there. Lindsey looked at me and told me I knew what I needed in my life. When I told her through tears that I didn't, she calmly reassured me that I did. On my drive home that day, and the days after, I sat and thought about what it was that I truly wanted.

I had been learning more about myself, building my boundaries and restructuring what I knew about myself, and every day showed me more of what I needed. When I told Lindsey I didn't know what I needed, it was because I had lost trust in myself and my decision-making abilities. How could I know what I wanted when the things that I thought I wanted ended up gone, bad, tragic or worse? There is no possible way to know what will go right in your life and what will not.

All this time, I had been telling myself that I didn't know what I wanted, and after going through this process, I realized that there was a fear of getting what I wanted and having it taken away from me. This reminds me of the people who say they are searching for, and are trying to find, true happiness. They feel that it is elusive when the reality is that it is right around the corner. You just have to look.

What have you been taught about happiness? Is true happiness having everything that you ever wanted in life? Or is it looking at what you have and feeling blessed and grateful? Only you know the answer to that question even if right now you don't feel it.

Through this journey, I have found my path to happiness, and I experience it every day. In 2023, I took a chance and got to see myself more clearly than I ever had. I stopped drinking so that I could focus on my relationships, financial wellness, career, and self-fulfillment. I took measures every day to make sure that I learned something new about myself. I learned what was holding me back. I let go of people, places and things that did not make me smile or make my heart sing. Happiness is not just about the amount of money that I make or the material things in my life. It is about how fully I can live every moment.

There is a story about an author who as a teen loved to read science fiction books but was told that they were for little kids. For years they stopped reading science fiction books and when they got older, they thought why? They loved them and wanted to read them, so they picked them up again. This reminds me of my ex who once told me "You know, you can just go to the store and get a birthday cake on any day of the week, and no one will be able to stop you. Do they check to see if it's your birthday when you buy the cake? No. You just buy it."

This can be true with a lot of the things people like. There may be people out there telling you that you can't do something because it's for "someone else". But who said that people can't do certain things? Who decided the age requirement on things in life? Now, I do not suggest taking a baby skydiving, or anything like that, but a 60-year-old may want to go to a trampoline or skate park. Who says they can't do it? Who made that rule?

There are a lot of things that I like to do as an adult that I am glad to be able to do. Truly being an adult is fun. Yes, there are consequences to most actions, but if you want ice cream for dinner or want to have a picnic in your front yard, who is going to stop you?

I started writing this book in a tent I put up in my backyard during Labor Day weekend in 2023. My neighbors were outside having a party next door with friends and family, and I painted in my backyard, started a fire in my firepit and set up my tent. Did they have hushed conversations about the weird neighbor who camped out in her backyard? Probably. But guess what? What does that have to do with me? I had a blast, and I was so happy to be in nature. That was probably the most time that I spent back there and I loved every single second. What do you want to do that will make your heart sing? I challenge you to make it happen in the next seven days.

Our lives are full of ups and downs, and each time, we're told to get back up to fight another day. There are things that we have forgotten, lost or put up on the shelf because other people said so or we thought that someone would think a certain way about us. The moment you sit back and look at what you want in your life, and you forget about who you are pretending to be, you will realize that there are a lot of things that you want to start back up again.

Activity: Make a list of things that you used to do as a kid that brought you joy. After you write out the list, pick a few things that you let go of that you wish you hadn't. Every week, pick one of those activities from your list to do. After you have done the activity, write about the activity, how it made you feel to do it again, and if you would continue to do it.

My friend, Jason, was talking to me about his life and when we got on the topic of what he liked to do, he said that he didn't know. He had gotten married and was now divorced. He became the residential parent of his child and worked to make sure that everything was taken care of. He spent almost twelve years of his life working and creating a life for his son, that he didn't take time to keep his own spark alive. I don't want this to happen to you. I know that my life is different from yours but answer me this. Do you believe that your life should be fulfilling?

When it came to my life and what I truly wanted things to look like, I started in one area: my career. I broke this down and thought about what it would look like, feel like, smell like, taste like and sound like. Why not? I wrote in my journal what I wanted in my career. I described in detail what a day in that life would look like. These scenes are mini manifestations of what I want and how I want to live. The who, what, when, where and how in technicolor.

On this journey, one of the last things I had to figure out was how to love myself again. I sat in my NET therapist's office, and I told her through tears that I did not know how to love myself or what I needed to show myself love. Once again, her message was the same, "yes you do."

As I continued on this journey, I found out what I loved, how I loved, and what I wanted to do to show myself love. I began to see that what I had been giving to others I could give to myself and that felt very different, almost selfish. It took time for me to realize that my healing journey started so that I could be the best me and be there for the people in my life. The important thing that I had to learn was how to not give all of myself away to another person.

After my soul death, I felt well enough to give to others. I started slowly, and even with all the work I did, I still felt depleted. It didn't feel as dramatic as before, but I needed to know how I could give and continue to fill myself. It was as if I needed two cups, one for me to fill and one for others to fill. Once I established that, I had to learn to fill my cup and use others to fill my cup so that I could replenish at the same time I gave.

How Do You Know When You Are Listening To Your True Self?

Before I decided to move into Transformation and Spiritual coaching, I was a Trauma Release Guide. I helped women who had been through trauma, specifically sexual trauma, so they could live their life authentically and release the stagnant energy that kept them from living their purpose. As the years went by, I did more research to learn other methods of helping my clients.

I talked to other coaches who helped people with trauma, and they suggested that I read *The Body Keeps the Score* by Bessel van der Kolk. I bought a copy of the book and started working my way through it. As I did, I realized that the book comes from a scientific point of view. They discuss what trauma does to the brain, how people experience their situations differently, and where trauma sits in the brain. The book also discusses effective methods that help people work through their trauma.

Throughout my healing journey, I have tried multiple methods to help me reconnect with my body after the trauma that I experienced as a little girl. A lot of those methods were in the book. How did I know what to do without going to therapy or a specialist for so long? Even though we need a bit of guidance when it comes to healing, our body and mind know exactly what it needs to heal. A big part of healing is listening.

I hear so often that people do not know where to start when they are starting their healing journey. To be honest, there is not one starting point because it depends on where the person is. We can start by understanding where we are right now and what it is that we are trying to accomplish. When I started my chakra journey, I could feel in my gut that that was the right place to start. I had the same feeling with yoga, pole fitness, and reading certain self-help books. Each of those methods taught me to pay attention to my body even when I didn't know it was speaking to me.

During my chakra alignment, everyday meditation was used to help me listen to my body, mind, and spirit. It is a way to help you focus your mind and listen to your intuition. You know that little voice in your head that tells you not to do something or that gut feeling that something is about to go wrong? That is your intuition. Meditating is a good start if you want to get more intimate and deeper with yourself and start to focus on listening to your inner voice.

There is a lot of misinformation about meditating, what it is and what it's supposed to look like. I've hosted a Meditation and Reiki Healing Workshop for almost a year and the people who attend sometimes tell me that they cannot sit still for too long, they get anxious when they close their eyes, they think too much when they aren't doing anything else, and so on. The biggest misconception about meditation is that you should clear your mind of all thoughts that exist. To this, I tell people, scientists say we think about 50,000 thoughts a day, I am sure that they do not stop when we slow down a bit.

Meditation is about understanding the inner dialogue of your mind and seeing the underlying sections of a thought and not just the surface. It is about calming your mind and paying attention to the thoughts that matter.

Think of it as watching the cars go by on the freeway. You are not watching one car go in the distance, you are picking out numerous cars and noticing them passing by. You watch for the speed they are going, or you see that one is driving erratically. You notice that there are far more dark-colored cars than light ones. That is how you view your thoughts in meditation. When a thought comes up multiple times, take note of it, breathe in, breathe out, and then move on to the next one. Meditation can be used as a way to process thoughts, emotions, and situations.

When you sit with yourself and meditate, you begin to learn who you are, how you think, the things that bother you the most and so much more. For many, sitting with themselves can be very hard. Most of us are used to ripping and running all the time. We're used to tending to other people's needs before our own and when we finally do sit down for a bit of peace and quiet, the last thing that we want to do is focus on ourselves and what it is that we need in that moment. I implore you to do just that.

To debunk another thing about meditating, I want to reassure you that you do not have to meditate for an hour for it to be effective. When I first started meditating, I was only doing ten-minute sessions. When I feel like I don't have the time to sit for ten minutes, I will take a minute or two to sit with myself. Any amount of time that you use to sit with yourself and be present in that moment, is time well spent.

I work with people who have never meditated before and ones who cannot sit still for long periods of time, and I tell them to start with two to five minutes a day. This helps them to take a second and breath. It gives them a chance to focus on their breath, releasing any restless energy that they have and then get back to their day. There is so much to learn about yourself, and it doesn't have to take 30 minutes of meditating to do it. Don't put so much pressure on yourself.

As you go through your journey of healing and changing, you will begin to hear your body speak. You will know when something is off or when you need to add an activity to your routine.

In the summer of 2019, a friend of mine convinced me to run the *Spartan* with him. The *Spartan* is a test of will and strength. There are three different obstacle courses of varying lengths, and each has a different number of obstacles included. I knew I wasn't in terrible shape, but I did think that if I did it, I would probably die. When I told my friend this, he said that I would be alright. I was not too sure about that.

Seven weeks before the race, I got an email from the company with a five-week workout plan. It was designed for any person who didn't work out to be able to complete a beginner *Spartan* race. The workout was five days a week, and included lunges, jogging, squats, crab walks, you name it. For those five weeks, I worked through the routines and if I missed a day, I would make sure to work out the next day. I was determined to finish the race and not die.

As I continued to work out, I noticed that my body would crave salad or vegetables right after. As it continued to happen more often, I realized that our bodies know exactly what it needs to grow muscle, bring up our energy levels, and take care of themselves. We just have to listen. The same thing happens when you are healing. Your body, your mind, and your intuition will tell you exactly what it is that you need.

One of the trauma coaches that I spoke with during my online summit referenced a story about her healing during our interview. She said that as she began to work on the processes of healing, one of the methods that she used was movement. Movement helped her to connect to her body in a more physical way. She felt so disconnected from herself and her physical self, that she could not physically connect with the sensation of her body. She told me that at one point, she was not able to tell where her foot was. She knew that it was connected to her ankle, which was connected to her lower leg, which was connected to her thigh, and she still could not make the actual connection to her body. Then she started yoga, and overtime she was able to connect to her foot once again.

Everybody is different. There are methods that work best for some and not for others. On Tik Tok, at the time of writing this book, there was a lot of talk about magnesium spray and how it helps with sleeping better, anxiety, restlessness and many other things. You had people who would rant and rave about the product, then you would have a few people who would say, well it didn't work for me. The creator would explain that one reason the product may not have worked for them is that they may already have an efficient amount of magnesium in their system, so it may not be the lack of magnesium causing their particular ailment.

This same thing can be said for vitamins as well. Charlotte got blood work done and she was told that her labs showed she needed more Vitamin D in her system. Instead of getting a vitamin specifically for Vitamin D, she decided to get a multi-vitamin that also had Vitamin D. When she started to take the vitamin, she would become ill. This story reminded me of my mom and why she would always get sick after eating liver. Liver has high iron content, and my mom had more than enough iron in her body. When she ate it, her body would reject it. It was the same thing that was happening with Charlotte. She needed Vitamin D, but because the multi-vitamin had a plethora of different vitamins in it, it was possible that it was giving her too much of the ones that she already had. Think about this when you decide to use topical or medicinal approaches to healing, or even when you are deciding what physical methods to use for healing. What does *your* body need?

Journaling: The Window To Your Thoughts

Journaling became a big part of my life at the beginning of my healing journey. Over the last fifteen years, I have journaled on and off. During the process of healing and resetting in 2023, I not only needed a way to get my thoughts out, but I also wanted to keep track of the emotions, and the changes that were sure to happen. To make it easy on myself, I used one journal and tried not to veer from that one space to write. That one journal carried all the thoughts that were going on in my brain, and I filled it up in the first three months of the year. By the end of 2023, I had filled almost four journals.

At the beginning, I would carry my journal with me everywhere in case I had something on my mind or needed to release. If I did not have my journal with me, I would take notes and then write in my journal later. Taking the time out to write down my thoughts would give me the time I needed to process what I was feeling and thinking. I personally feel there is something powerful about the pen-to-paper method of journaling. For me, there is a deeper connection when my thoughts travel from my head to my hand and on that sheet of paper. Of course, you are welcome to use a physical journal or an electronic journal to get started. Neither method works better than the other.

There are people who don't like to write, or they seldomly write, and are wondering, "well, what do I write about?" The answer is everything!!

For the first three months, I wrote about my journey of not drinking and getting up early. I wrote about my emotions and why I thought that not drinking was a good idea. I wrote about all the things that I was doing to move forward in my life, and all the thoughts I had about situations that bothered me. I wrote about the triggers in my life that still made me want to drink. I wrote about what triggered me that day and how I wanted a drink. I would write about what I did when I got up that morning. I wrote about how I was feeling and sometimes I would free write about whatever came to my mind. My thoughts often came out disjointed, or they would be clear streams of consciousness. As time went on, I became better at managing my thoughts and processing my emotions.

If you are not sure what to write about, you can use journal prompts to help you. To help journaling become a habit, start a five-to-ten-minute timer, pick a journal prompt, and write what comes to mind.

Journaling helps me analyze my thoughts and emotions. It allows me to see exactly how my mindset has changed since I started my journey, and my day-to-day living. I have written journal entries cursing out my exes and journal entries that talk about the deepest, darkest parts of me. Sometimes the thoughts we hold onto in our heads are the heaviest burden we bear.

If you want to dive a bit deeper into journaling, you will find that it helps to see what triggers you in any given situation. When we are amid a heated debate and we are trying to work it out right then, sometimes we cannot pinpoint what it is that is triggering us. Is it the fact that your co-worker yelled at you? Or is it the fact that you felt as if they weren't listening, and it reminded you of your childhood? These things are important building blocks to understand who you are and how you can get out of your own way. You also start to realize what methods help you to see clearly in situations of high tension. When you take the time to replay the situation and analyze it, like a scientist, you start to see patterns that you continue to do.

Remember, journaling looks different for everyone. You can determine how often you write in your journal, whether it be once a day, twice a week, or a few times a month. It can be quotes or song lyrics, the dreams of your future self, a novel of thoughts that go on for 40 pages… yes, I wrote a 40-page journal entry once. Journaling helps you to get closer to yourself. You will write things that you did not know existed in your brain and you will start to see what lies beneath is not always a bad thing, but a door to your inner truth.

Journal Prompt: Why did I pick up this book? What about this book attracting me to reading it? As I continue to read through the chapters, what have I learned about myself?

Celebration: Carve out time once a month to do a fun activity on your list. You can do it more often, but this is just a start. Hold yourself to it, then continue to add more activities each month that you like. Live like yourself again. If you have a family, bring them into the fold as well. Help them to understand that when they are happy, life feels better.

Reason #9

Because Alcohol Has Been My Substitute For The Love And Connection I Actually Want

Alcohol As Counterfeit Connection

I realized today that this book is a living, breathing piece of work. Although I wrote the outline and second draft in six months, I continue to go through my next year of transformation. I am still growing, and I am starting to understand myself more and more every day.

When I started writing this book, I was not opening myself up to creating new relationships, platonic or romantic. Even though I am polyamorous, the breakup I had in March of 2023 took a lot out of me. I was still with my boyfriend, who continued to be there for me through that time, but adding more people into my romantic life, sounded exhausting. Hell! Finding new friends or hanging out with people was exhausting. I was not ready to build connections at all. How was I going to write about something that I was in the process of starting over for myself?

One year and eight days after my breakup, I went on a trip that put me face-to-face with my ex. A friend of mine hosts a casino trip every year around the end of March. I saw the trip come up and I did not have any plans, so I called my friend and asked if there were spaces left for the trip. He told me they did, so I bought a seat.

Because I met this friend through my ex, I knew that there was a possibility that she was going to be there. I didn't do anything to prepare myself for what was going to happen next.

I walked into the meeting space at 7:00 a.m. that morning and talked to everyone. When my ex entered the room, she said hi and I said hi back. We then went our separate ways. As we loaded onto the bus, my ex and I ended up sitting in seats diagonally from one another, but we didn't say a word. I did not think that we were going to talk, so I pulled out my book and started to read on this three-hour bus ride to Seneca, New York.

Once we arrived at the casino, we all got instructions on our free play and what time to be back on the bus, and everyone got off. I spent most of the morning wandering around by myself and enjoying the atmosphere. As I walked through the casino, my ex and I walked right into one another's path. We sparked a conversation and started to talk about how we were doing and the things that were going on in our lives. We were then interrupted by a friend who needed help finding her stuffed llamacorn, a mix of a llama and unicorn, Chardonay, Char-Char for short, so we disbursed and began our search. I ended up finding Char-Char at the lost in found, and the day was saved. I hung out with my friend for a bit and waited until it was time for us to leave.

As we boarded the bus to head home, I looked over for a chance to talk to my ex. She pulled out a book, and started reading, so I continued to read my book for a bit.

About an hour into the bus ride, I looked over and my ex was not reading or napping, so I took my chance. I got up and slid into the seat next to her. We started talking and that conversation led to us talking about our relationship, why it ended and gaining a sense of closure. We talked about things that should have been discussed at the time and how we each felt that the other was losing interest. As we continued to chat, there was a point that I shared with her that I stopped feeling emotions for a couple months after our breakup, which also led to me not listening to music. She was very surprised by this.

As we discussed it more, the weight on my heart lifted completely when I blurted out that my emotions stopped because I didn't want to give her love away to anyone else. That blew my mind! All that time that I had been writing in my journal, going to NET therapy, and talking to my friends, I never thought of that. It was not until I saw her, talked to her, and was able to truly express my feelings, that I was able to figure out why I stopped all of my emotions in the first place.

Not everyone is able to get closure, and in some situations, I believe that closure is not warranted. In my situation, the closure I gained from this interaction helped me to reset my heart and open my heart again not only to my emotions, but to love as well. And that is how this chapter even came to be, so thank you, Universe, for allowing that closure to happen.

I look back at my friendships and relationships before I stopped drinking, and it amazes me how much has changed. I had more friends in my life who drank and when I hung out with them, I drank more. I wanted to be on the same level they were, and I wanted to "have fun". I did have friends that didn't drink, and even when I hung out with them, I drank. Sometimes it was because I wanted to and other times it was because I felt like I needed it to liven up the party.

The first few months of my journey were the hardest, and the people that I called my friends would still invite me out. Some dared to ask me if I would be able to keep from drinking while I was out. It didn't take much willpower because I was on a mission. I never realized that the friendships that I had created with some of those friends was only because I drank. We may have had some things in common, but the one think that was consistent was that we liked to drink, and bitch and complain. The very things that I was trying to get rid of.

The question here is how do you want to reconnect with the people around you or with new people? Are you open to new platonic or romantic relationships that no longer involve drinking? What do you have to let go of before you begin to bring others into your life? Do we want love or do we simply want connection?

In the relationship with my ex, I felt that I gave my all and felt like I was shafted in the end. I was giving my love and attention to someone who I knew could not or would not give back to me. I knew up front what this person was capable of emotionally and I decided to ignore it and do it anyway. That's what love is right?

Connections aren't meant to feel fake or forced. They should come naturally and genuinely. Think about the relationships you created during a period when you were knee deep in unhealthy habits and patterns. What types of shenanigans did you get into? How did these people enable your behavior?

Think about what happens to those people when you're no longer drinking. I know I didn't. I wasn't ready for the number of "friends" I would lose because I stopped that one action. However, that gave me time to think about what I really wanted in connection and love.

Are You Emotionally Available?

When it comes to relationships, what are you looking for? Have you thought about whether you are emotionally ready to take on a new relationship?

A good place to start your new relationship journey is asking yourself what you don't want in a relationship or friendship. I had a conversation with Lindsey who told me that before she found her husband, she wrote down all the things that she did not want first and then she wrote down the opposite of those things. This does not mean that you need to know the name of the exact person that you want to be with. It goes deeper than that. A lot of times, people think about the surface level things that they want. They want someone with brown eyes, black hair, soft medium sized lips, a round nose, and a symmetrical face. They want someone who has a shapely body, active, has sex daily, and a nice paying job. This person will help take care of bills, and the list goes on and on. Newsflash!! Someone with these qualities could still treat you like shit. This person could also treat you like royalty, but you would still find flaws within them. Don't focus on the idea of them. First, you must know what you are looking for. What are the qualities in the person or people that you want in your life? What are their beliefs? Their values? Do they complement your own or are they completely opposite?

After her divorce four years ago, Nikki dipped her toe back into the dating game. When she got divorced, she went to therapy to work through the failure that she felt as a wife and as a mother. She felt that she was not ready for another relationship until she knew exactly what she wanted in her romantic relationships and how not to drag the other person down with her baggage.

There are some people who curse relationships while also trying to chase a relationship. There are some people who go right into a relationship after they get out of one so that they are not alone. There are others who take a while before getting back into the dating scene. Then there are those who decide that they want to be alone for the rest of their life because of the work it takes to be in a relationship. Nikki fit into the category of not wanting to be alone, and also not wanting to settle.

Nikki was talking to her friend about what she was looking for. In her heart of hearts, she was someone who loved love. Her desire was to give love and to receive love. When she talks about the person that she wants to end up with, she talks about the amount of care that she gives to people and how she wants it to be reciprocated. She doesn't give love for the expectation of getting anything back. However, like with any relationship, we want to know that the person we are with cares for us as much as we care for them. It's not about love equality, but about love equity. We want someone to show us that they care about us.

When you make the decision to get back into the dating or friend world, you have to take a step back, look at the battlefield, your heart, and assess the damage. How did you get here? What was done to cause this destruction? What things need to change? How do you heal so that you do not take your baggage into your next relationship?

Remember that nothing is off limits in your world. You have the power to create the life that you want, and you get to choose who you want in it. Have faith that the world that you are creating will be what you want and know that you do not have control over another person's actions, words, and understanding of life. We are all here to learn about the things that other people have to offer and how they can change your life for the good or for the bad.

You have to ask yourself: What is your goal for a relationship or friendship? What are the traits that you want and don't want in that person? How do you want this person to approach you?

For example, if you are ready to start dating, and you don't have a partner, the first thing that you can do is start dating yourself. There are people in this world who have no idea who they are because they have spent too much time focusing on other people in their lives. You cannot know what you want and don't want, if you don't sit with yourself and learn who you are. So, plan a date. If you were someone who was interested in you, what type of date would you plan? Take a moment and write out the date. What day of the week will you be taking yourself out, and what time? What are you going to wear? Plan an activity and a meal. Don't skimp on yourself either.

On the day that you take yourself out, think about how this person treats you as they take you out. What things will you talk about or explore? Remember all the details. When your date is over, go home and take a moment to write out how that date felt. What the expectation was, and what happened. What are things that you wish had happened? Then make a list of the traits of the person that you could see yourself with in the future.

Understand that everything you do in life is a risk, you just have to decide, is it worth it? In love, there is always a risk. You will put your heart on the line for another person, all for the romance of a fairy tale love. In life and in your relationships, you want to take risks often. Nikki took a huge risk by getting back out into the dating world. She did not know what she was going to find or who she was going to run into, but you learn from doing. The risks in love cannot be calculated. You will never know where you will end up, in love or in life, if you don't step out of your comfort zone and try. In taking risk, you learn what you need to know about the world, about decisions, and about choices. You have control over your actions. You will not be happy in the same place if you choose to do nothing.

As you dream of what you want, be selfish. Think of this list as your Genie. The order you put in with the Universe will be cooked up and brought to you. It is not about perfection, but about who you can see yourself with, what you want from that dream life, and what you are going to do for it.

If you know what you want, you will never accept less than that.

The ever-important question is are you ready?

Creating the People We Want In Our Lives

Darren Hardy, the founder of *Success Magazine*, describes how he manifested his wife. He explains that he wrote a 40-page description of who his wife was which included what she looked like, how she talked, what she did for a living and so on. He wrote everything that he could think of down in those pages and "as if she were peeled right off those pages," his wife came into his life.

In the movie *Practical Magic*, Sally uses this same principle to create a man that she would fall in love with. Their family suffered from a curse that whoever they fell in love with would be doomed to die. In her spell, she gave the love of her life features that she believed no one could have. To her, it assured her that she would never fall in love.

Later, while making a spell to banish a detective, her daughters find the spell and ask their aunt if it was written about their dad. At first, their aunt Gillian lies and says it was, but when her nieces correct her about their father's eye color, she tells them that their mom made up the spell so that she would not fall in love. As Sally's daughters watch the detective, they realize that he is the man from their mom's spell, and they decide not to banish him.

Saying that you want someone who is not in a fraternity, doesn't drink or do hard drugs, and doesn't have children are not sufficient. These were the only details that I used when I started dating in college. True story! I didn't have any other details about the person who I wanted to be with, but I did not heed my own preferences. I actually ran face first into them. My ex-husband happened to be in a fraternity and when we eventually got together, he had a newborn son. The only thing that he didn't do was drink in excess. At the time, I felt that he was the perfect one for me, but there were a lot of details about what I wanted in a husband that I didn't think about. Do you see how very little information that gives the Universe or any higher power to work with?

Terri and her friend, Grant, went to an art installation at a museum in a nearby town. Grant was celebrating his birthday and invited her along because he knew that she liked museums. With it being a new installation, they were going to see different contemporary art pieces, and they knew that there were going to be interactive art pieces as well.

They first hung outside the museum since there was a DJ and food trucks. They walked around, vibing to the music and talking excitedly about what they expected inside. They walked inside the museum and started viewing the art on the first floor.

As they walked to each floor, Terri stopped on a floor where they had an interactive exhibit. As she walked into this room, there were strings, clothespins, and notes pinned along the wall. She walked over to the wall and started to read the notes. She saw that there were notes to friends, poems, and short stories written on these notes. Each one from someone who came though the museum. She turned to the tables where she found paper, fabric, rope, colored pencils, pens, and markers. Seeing the notes gave her a great idea to write a letter to the future love of her life. She thought about what she was missing in her life and who the future love of her life would be. She thought about how they would treat her, how she would treat them, and what she was looking for. She wrote down things that she would say to them and how they would interact with one another. Then she took a picture of the paper and hung it on the wall, leaving it to the world and the Universe.

I know in this section I talk about finding romantic relationships. This same method can be used to find your tribe.

When Sam moved into a new neighborhood, they were looking for like-minded people to explore this world with. They knew that they wanted to grow and be present, and they wanted to have community. Being new in town, they didn't know much about the area. They sat down one afternoon and thought about what they wanted from the communities they would join. They wrote it down in detail and they thought about it constantly.

One day, while scrolling through Eventbrite, they found an event that they thought looked interesting and signed up. When they showed up to the event, they introduced themselves to the hostess and other attendees and soon realized that this was exactly what they were looking for.

Exercise: Take a moment to do as Mr. Hardy, Sally, Terri, and Sam did. Create the person, community, or friend of your dreams. Write out what this person or people would be like. What would they look like? How would they treat you, your family and friends, and people on the street? What job would they have? Do they have their own home? Do they take care of their own finances? How is their relationship with their family? Think about every single aspect that you can when it comes to your dream partner. Once you put it down on paper, or in electronic form, read it, visualize them, and feel the emotions that come up when you think of your person or people. The only rules are to not put a name to them or the face of someone you know. Dream this person up from scratch. It is all about imagination and intention.

Remember as you are writing down the traits of people you want to attract, include as much detail as you can. Darren Hardy left no stone unturned when he wrote out his 40-page description, and you shouldn't either. If you are thinking, do I have to write 40 pages? The answer is no. It can be as long or as short as you want it to be, as long as there are details.

Who Are You Becoming Without Alcohol (Or Unhealthy Habit)

The next step in the process is becoming the person that you've wanted to be without the unhealthy habit. This whole journey is about learning who you are and how you want to live your life. Understand that you are not able to build connections with others if you do not know who you are to begin with. This is how people lose themselves in their relationships.

With any book we read or podcast that we listen to, we take in the information that we want and leave the rest. When I started my polyamorous journey, I had no idea what I was doing. It was like I came out of the fog that was my relationship and decided that I was going to start all over. I met a woman who ran a polyamorous group, and I wanted to attend a meeting because I was curious. I was a sexual health consultant at the time, and I thought it would be a different angle to come from when it came to learning about sexual desires, and understanding the different dynamics that people have in their relationships. Before I attended the meeting, I did some research and I knew that I was poly.

I went to the meeting, and I had a good time talking to everyone and learning their stories. I asked the hostess for some resources, and she gave me the name of a book. I read one and a half books about polyamory and listened to about 200 episodes of a poly podcast, and I learned a lot about myself, people, and relationships.

While listening to the podcast, the hosts talked about creating an "instruction manual" for the person that you are dating. They suggested that once you created this manual that you share it with the person that you are dating as a way to help them get to know you. You would define what a relationship is to you and what type of person you are in a relationship. You get into the intimate details of your life that you never told anyone, and it helps you to explore the qualities about yourself that you admire, and others that you never thought to highlight.

Although it was intended to help others learn more about you, I decided to turn it into a guide to understanding myself. Instead of creating an instruction manual, I decided to create a self-discovery manual. This manual focuses on who you were, who you want to be and who you are becoming. I started it as a way for sexual trauma survivors to understand themselves through their healing journey and after their experience. It helps to guide people through different journals and question prompts that help them in their relationships. They gain understanding about how they want to be treated, and how to discover and deal with their triggers. It helps you focus on the things that you hold dear and shed light on the things that need to change.

Exercise: Start creating your own instruction manual. Start by describing who you are right now, what you do for a living, your habits, etc. As you write out this description, think about what your dream partner is looking for in a partner, and what your dream community looks like. Write those qualities, traits, and features down. This may not take 40 pages, but it could be. Remember, this description is of who *you* want to be, not who *other person* want you to be. A change made solely for someone else is not going to be a lasting change.

Once you get a good picture of who you want to be in life and in your relationships, then you start to make the changes. The biggest reason I stopped drinking was because I was not dealing with my problems head on. I was drowning in them. Another reason I stopped drinking was because I liked how I felt around my boyfriend, who didn't drink. We always had a great time, and I didn't feel like I had to drink with him around.

Make sure that you are excited for your outcome. The rush of excitement that you will feel when you have your dream life will not compare to anything you have ever felt. How long are you willing to put the life that you want on the backburner, before you get to be truly happy?

Take the leap and make the changes.

I know that in relationships, I am a romantic at heart. I also romanticize my friendships as well. I adore the people I surround myself with and I know that I will go above and beyond for them. Once that relationship gets going, I don't stop being there for them. I'll give you an example.

During the beginning of the pandemic, the world was shut down. This ruined a lot of plans for people who wanted to travel. My ex and I included. We were planning to go to the Word Museum in Washington, D.C. Yes! A museum of words. When the pandemic hit, that trip was cancelled, and we were both disappointed. It was one of the first trips that I was planning for her birthday, and because of that I wanted to do something special for her in place of it.

I came up with the idea of doing an art museum at my house. I figured since we couldn't go anywhere, I would bring the museum to her. I created a theme for the museum, and I created about a dozen art pieces. For almost two weeks, I worked on this project. I painted the pieces, named them and even made tags for the pictures, like you would see in a museum. We would see each other as I was putting this together, so I hid all the pictures in the basement.

As this special weekend approached, I got nervous. I had dinner planned out. I went to the Metroparks where I picked flat rocks for us to do rock paintings. I even talked to her niece about what I was planning and asked her whether or not she thought that my ex would like it. She loved the idea and knew that her aunt would love it.

A couple days before the weekend started, I wanted to do something a bit extra. I didn't want her to just come to my house and then wallah, she steps into the museum. My friend came up with the idea of driving her around the city and then taking her back to my house. It was definitely the "extra" that I was looking for and after some back and forth, I decided to do it.

Now keep in mind, my ex and I were not dating at this time, but I wanted to show her that I liked her, and I wanted to impress her. When she got to the house, I told her to get in the car. I gave her a blindfold, which she reluctantly put on. I pulled out of my driveway, and we were off! We took a 30-minute drive around the city and then came back to my house.

We pulled into my driveway, and I told her to take off her blindfold. When she did, she laughed. She told me that it was definitely something that she would have done, and she liked it. I handed her an envelope and inside was a picture that I had colored. On the back was a hangman game with a note. It talked about how we were supposed to do this "thing", but the pandemic ruined our plans. She guessed the answer correctly and we got out of the car and stepped to the front door. I asked her to choose one or two. She chose two and we walked into the house.

I told her to go explore the museum as I prepared option two. She walked around the dining room looking at all the pictures that I had created while I prepared our plates for dinner. I made her favorite meal, baked ziti, and we sat down to eat. We ate and talked about the art I created, and how it was a neat idea. After we ate, I cleared the table and pulled out the flat rocks I had collected. I found a tutorial on YouTube to paint rocks and had her choose which scene she wanted. She chose a beach scene, and we painted our rocks. It was probably the most romantic thing I had ever done for anyone.

When it comes down to who I am, I will always be a romantic.

Who are you going to be in your relationship?

As you explore your new sense of relationships and what you want, I want to leave you with some points of wisdom. As people who like things that are bad for us, which is everyone, we often fall into the same habits and traps when it comes to connecting with others. When you begin your search for community and for romance, remember these two lessons.

1. Listen when people tell you who they are.

Social media has a vast amount of information, videos, and memes of the actions of other people in any type of relationship. There are people who will be transparent and honest with you, people who will try to deceive you, and people who do not know what they want, let alone say what they want.

Love is an easy emotion. You want to believe what you hear and how you feel. Our idea of love can create a filter where we ignore what is being shown through their actions.

With my ex, I dealt with a person who told me exactly who she was, how she dealt with emotions, and the issues that she had in her past relationships. There was a part of me that wanted to love her, and then there was another part of me that wanted to try to fix her heart and help her get over the things that she held onto. The issue is that people who are not ready to fix their problems will continue doing what they do. They will not change their patterns. They will not change how they interact. They will not change how they feel towards relationships. This will continue until they decide that they want to change.

If a person is not ready to change, for themselves, they will "make" the changes for a short time and then go back to their old ways. The reason for this is that they only wanted to change for the other person and not for themselves. Even if there is positive reinforcement given in their change process, oftentimes they will revert to their original behaviors. You can want someone to change with all your heart, and when they are ready, they will.

When a person is ready to change for themselves, they will make the change because they will do it because of how their life makes them feel. These types of changes terms to last longer.

Listen to what they tell you about themselves and see if that is something you can deal with in a relationship or in a friendship. Do not try to force someone to change. You will only get short term results or none at all.

Do not ignore your instincts or ignore the things that anyone tells you. If they say something and it feels off, ask them or go with your gut. Do not continue to walk into red flags at the expense of yourself. There is nothing like trying to have a healthy relationship and being jaded at the same time.

2. Do not use people as a distraction.

When I went through my soul death and started to remove people who I did not want in my life, I realized that people will fill their time with others so they don't have to deal with their own shit.

Derek was having a rough time in his relationship with his boyfriend. They were both exploring an open relationship but had not dealt with their internal issues. Among many issues, there was a lack of trust that was never resolved. They stopped connecting with one another and anytime he brought up a conversation about it with his boyfriend, he would get shut down.

Since Derek was not able to talk with his boyfriend about the loneliness that he was feeling, his need to reconnect with him, and rebuild their trust, he decided to fill his time with other people and activities. He started to join apps where he could find new friends and possible relationships. With each step, his relationship with his partner was suffering. As they grew further apart, Derek tried to talk to more people, go on more dates, and invite people into his life. None of which worked.

After months of doing this and not finding anything that helped relieve the issues, Derek decided to look at his current relationship and figure out what were the underlying issues. As he did this, he realized that he had been trying to fill a void with another person. He wanted to spend time with his boyfriend, but since he was not available or never wanted to do so, Derek began to look elsewhere. The reason that the feeling did not go away is because you cannot fill a void with something that did not create the void. You are basically putting a Band-Aid on the problem, which doesn't last long.

In most major cities, you will find plenty of potholes. Some places will place gravel in the hole to temporarily "fix" the problem. Over time, the gravel will get kicked out of the hole by the tires and will cause the pothole to appear once again. The problem is repaired when a construction crew comes out and goes through the process of properly filling the hole. They will clear the pothole of any debris. They then overfill the hole with a cold-patch material or asphalt. The material is spread out over the hole to make sure the pocket is filled. They will then bring out a tool to help them compact the material. Then, and only then, has the pothole been properly repaired.

Once Derek realized that the people and activities that he was engaging in were a distraction, he decided that he was going to work on himself, get out of the relationship that was not fulfilling his needs, and find what he truly wanted in a relationship. He had to decide, does he want to bring someone else into his baggage, or does he want to deal with it first?

These two lessons will help you navigate all the new relationship energy that will happen as you find your person and your people. You don't have to be too cautious, but you do want to make sure you are not falling into those same patterns.

Reason #10

Because Deep Down, I'm Afraid To Believe I Deserve More Than Survival

Breaking Up With Survival Mode

Before Jasmine's divorce, she started planning for the inevitability of being alone and taking care of the household bills by herself. Her relationship was falling apart, and she thought about what would happen if her spouse were to leave her in a lurch. She had been working part-time for almost a year and loved the freedom it gave to her, but she knew that if things were to change in her living situation, she would have to pay all the bills. She thought about whether she was able to handle it on her current pay, or if she would drown in mountains of late bills. Although she did not want to work full-time, she had to think about what was best for her in that position.

Instead of waiting for her partner to leave and having to deal with the aftermath of scrambling to make ends meet, she spoke to her boss and asked if the full-time position was available to her. When they asked her why she was looking for a full-time position, she explained to them that her circumstances had changed, and a full-time position would help her immensely. They understood and gave her the full-time position.

When she later switched jobs, she worked like her life depended on it. Her income took a dip and even with overtime capabilities, she was maintaining her head above water, and not by much.

After a couple of years working at the new firm, she talked to her best friend. Jasmine talked to her best friend almost every day. She knew what

Jasmine was going through. Jasmine would often stay late at work to get overtime, and worked hard to make ends meet. While they were talking, her best friend stopped her and said, "Jasmine, you are still working as if you are in survival mode, and you're not." Oof! That knocked the very wind out of Jasmine's chest. She had never thought about it before, and she knew that her best friend was right.

For three years, Jasmine had been working her ass off living what most people know as "paycheck-to-paycheck". Even though she was no longer struggling like she was at the beginning process of her divorce, she was still operating like she was. Killing herself to make sure she didn't fall back into the same financial situation she was left in.

Part of our journey with bad habits is understanding that in order to get out of survival mode, we must get a better handle on our situation, money and the actions that we take with it. Like most people, we are used to thinking about money when something major happens and we need to do something immediately to fix it. It was not a forethought and honestly, when all you know is survival, taking care of money is not something we think about. Jasmine proactively thought about her situation and came up with a plan that would not put her into debt, or worse.

There have been plenty of times in my life where I only reacted to my financial situation. I did not really pay attention to how money flowed in and out of my home. I sure would not have realized that I was staying in the same mindset that I did when all I could think about was survival.

I started to take a closer look at my finances when a friend of mine came to visit me a few weeks after my devastating breakup. She had never been to my house, so when she saw it, she instantly fell in love with it and called me rich the entire time she was here. She not only said that I was rich, she called me a millionaire! For two days, she never stopped telling me that. In this moment, I knew I needed to change my mindset around money. I started to ask myself, what do rich people do with their money? How do they handle their money? What do I need to do to earn a million dollars and how can I use that to make my life financially easy and stable?

As these questions floated around in my head, I remembered that many years ago, I received a ton of resources surrounding mindset, money, and business. I dug into my resources and found the *Gratitude Journal for Money* by Tasha Chen. This journal helps you deep dive into your relationship with money, your thoughts around money, how you use money, and how you feel about money. This 30-day journal helps you uncover things about money that you may not have realized you were holding onto, and it helps you shift your mindset.

One of the biggest mindset shifts I made was allowing money access to my life. Many people have resistance to money for a number of reasons. It could be their upbringing, their beliefs, and the amount of money they have in their accounts right now. There are some people who believe that being rich and wealthy has nothing to do with money at all. There are people who have less money and feel richer than all the people in the world.

Breaking up with survival mode is not only about money, but also about the mindset that you have around your life, where you are and what you can do. When we are only surviving, we often cannot think past where we are now. We only think about what led us to this place and how we deserve what we have. The reality is that we want so much more. We have to realize where we are and know that it is something that can be changed, even if we created the circumstances that we are currently living in. We don't have to stay where we are, especially if we really want to grow and thrive.

Rebuilding After Chaos

Rebuilding after chaos takes confidence. Educating yourself on topics that you don't understand is important and necessary especially when you are talking about finances.

When I started my network marketing business, David Bach came to a conference and spoke to the consultants. He talked about retirement and how to save money. Years later, I found influencer Tori Dunlap, the Financial Feminist, and listened to the steps she took to make her first $100k. In your search for rebuilding, find someone who speaks to you and your situation. Devour their content by reading their books, listening to their podcasts, or watching their YouTube channel. Then, take small steps to create the wealth that you desire.

I started by using the Gratitude Journal for Money and shifted my mindset about money. Living in survival mode for so long, I only had the skills to make sure I didn't fall behind. I needed the skills to learn how to spend differently, how to save differently, and how to see money as a resource. Wanting something better for yourself and doing something better for yourself are two different things.

Maybe you want to save $100,000. Maybe you want to make sure groceries are paid for every month and have a bit extra for a snack you love. Only you can determine that.

Survival mode kept me from asking for more money when I switched jobs. For years, I would take what the company offered me because they said it was "capped". I believed them and never asked for more. Then my situation got turned on its head and I realized that I needed to do something different with my finances if I wanted to feel like I wasn't drowning.

I thought to make more money, I had to leave my job for a better paying one, or better opportunities. The jobs that I had had no growth potential, so it made sense to find another one. Since I started working out of college, I was used to getting a pay cut when I started a new job. I thought that was what I had to do to get my foot in the door and show them what I could do. I realize now that I was also reacting to my situation and was trying to move immediately, so it felt like I didn't have a choice.

Before I decided to leave my last job, I decided that I would try to negotiate my salary. It was time that I stopped playing small, and that I asked for what I wanted and not be afraid. I talked to my two best friends and asked them if they had ever negotiated their salary. They told me yes and explained that they negotiated their salary *before* they got into their positions. I was blown away! Not only had I never done that before, but I had never once asked for a raise. They gave me lots of information on why they do this and how I can do research to get a raise myself. Of course, I took their advice. I went to YouTube University to learn how to negotiate my salary and I sat on it for weeks. Then I finally got up the courage to ask for a raise, and I got it! Over the next few years, I continued to negotiate my raises and when I left that job, I negotiated my new salary. By doing this, my income grew by 70% from 2019 to 2023.

Armed with this information, I helped others to become more confident in asking for a raise.

I worked with Mary who was struggling with the amount of money she earned and wanted to increase her pay. Her situation was very different from mine, as she was married and had children. Her and her husband both worked, and she said that they fell behind with bills, and funding their kids' activities.

She had been wondering what she should do and asked for my thoughts on her situation. I asked her if she ever thought about negotiating her salary. I think she may have been taken aback by the question. She had been working in the same position for four years and had never asked for a raise. There were other factors that kept her from doing so, and she took the annual raises and bonuses because she felt that she couldn't ask for more. She worked just as hard as I did and really wanted the pay and benefits that reflected it. I agreed to come by her home and talk to her about her options.

Seeing as I was no longer at the same workplace, we talked about her salary and what information she would need to negotiate her new terms. I explained to her how I figured out the numbers of what I wanted to earn and what I could earn based on the area, type of firm, and so on. We did an old-fashioned spreadsheet and got all the numbers that she wanted to discuss with the boss. We talked about vacation time, salary, and benefits that would help her feel more secure and not like her and her husband would continue to be behind.

When I checked on her months later, she told me that she got what she wanted when it came to vacation time, salary, and benefits.

It pays to weigh your options.

If you feel that you are not in the best financial situation, there is always a way to change it. Some people negotiate their salary. Others quit and find a new job. How do you know which one to choose?

When I feel like I am ready to quit a job, I start looking at reasons why someone would leave their job and if it is a good idea to do the same. You are learning how to move differently in your life and make decisions that fit where you want to go. You must think about the reasons that you are leaving your job and what you will do if you have to stay. The questions I would implore you to ask yourself as you are rebuilding your life are: What keeps me stuck here? Am I staying because I feel like I owe the people that I work for or am I staying because I really like my job? Do I wake up excited to go to work, or do I wake up and dread going to work? Ultimately, you will find all the reasons that you need to stay or go, and the reality is that you are the only one that can make that decision.

In 2018, I quit my job at the county prosecutor's office. I was getting paid decently. I liked what I did. My healthcare was included and free. It was a job that I felt secure in, but that was about it. Not only was I working full-time, I was also working my business part-time. After three years of being there, I became unhappy with where I was in my career. There was no growth potential in my office, and I wanted more.

One day, I sat and thought about where I was in my career and how I got there. At this time, I had been working since I graduated from college, and I really didn't know what I wanted to do with my life. We are taught to go to school, graduate, go to college, get a job, and work. I took a hard look at my life and realized that I had not really figured out who I was. I took a glimpse five years into the future, and saw that if I stayed in that position, I would still be unhappy, and I decided it was not worth it. I chose a random date on the calendar and decided that that was the day I would quit. I told a couple of people what I planned to do, and some of them were skeptical. As that date approached, I put in my two weeks. The decision is always yours, no matter what the reason is.

Rebuilding does not have to be hard, but it does have to be stable.

Building Stability You Don't Sabotage

I never knew that I wanted to be "financially free" until I started my network marketing business. It was a topic they talked about constantly and it made me realize that I needed to make some changes if I wanted to set myself up for wealth.

As I began to figure out my thoughts around financial freedom, talking to people about money and finding mentors, I started to see that there are many different plans to living abundantly.

Exercise: Take a look at where you are financially and where you want to be. What are your goals? Are you on track? If not, how can you get there? What are the steps you must take to get there? Create a plan and work the plan.

My overall goal was to have a better relationship and thought process surrounding money. Second, I wanted to save an emergency fund for at least six months. Third, I wanted to pay off the debts that I felt were holding me back.

To start this process, I was actively doing the *Gratitude Journal for Money*, and I discovered that my thoughts about money were holding me back. As I continued to work on my money mindset, I also looked at my money security. Oftentimes we have fears around losing money or not having enough. That doesn't bode well when you want to save money. So, we get those old money scripts out and plug in a new set of scripts that help one feel abundant.

The next step in this plan was to figure out how much I wanted in my emergency fund, how much I was going to save, and how those funds would be used. Most experts will tell you to start with $1,000 to $2,000 in your emergency fund. This will help to solidify the process of saving and show that you are capable. I planned to put $150 each paycheck into my savings account until I hit the first $1,000. Once that goal was complete, I would start taking the $150 and put it towards my debt to start paying it down. To help bring in a few extra dollars, I worked for my previous law firm as a contractor. That helped me to bring in about $350 extra biweekly.

When I started getting paid from my contracting job, I wanted to be able to fulfill my goals but also spend some money on myself. Living in survival mode often kept me from buying things for myself even if I needed them. The work I had done surrounding money showed me that I should not only use money for the necessities. It taught me that I am deserving of the money that I earn and it is good to spend money on ourselves.

To help manage the extra funds, my boyfriend taught me about the 50/30/20 rule. He explained that 50% of my funds would be used to pay off my debts, 30% would be used for savings, and the last 20% would be used for fun money. This same method can be used for your regular paycheck, extra checks, or bonuses. Of course, you can move the percentages up or down for your specific needs.

Here's the reality, no matter how you set up your finances, relationships, habits, and job, you want to make sure that it is built to be sustainable and comfortable. Coming out of a situation where we have let our addiction, co-dependence, or unhealthy habits run our lives can coax us back into the familiar and comfortable space of chaos and sabotage. Remember that you are human. You may fall back into those familiar patterns and that is okay. It is important that you give yourself grace and be kind. We are going to make mistakes. The new path we have created is unfamiliar and scary. Some days are going to be better than others and we are going to fall sometimes. When you feel down, remember your why, believe in the person you are becoming, and call on your support system. You are not alone in this journey.

Words to Guide You Into Your Next Chapter

I stopped drinking because I wanted to be a better me. Sometimes that takes being the bigger person in your life, growing up and putting your big person panties on. Life is too short to sit back and let everything else control who you are or what you do.

When will you decide to take your life back?

I hope that this book has taught you that you can take your life into your own hands and that no matter what decision you make, you know that you are making the right one for you. Life is about choices. Whether it is to sit and do absolutely nothing or whether it is to act. No one else can make the decisions for you. You have to do it.

This book is designed for you to read, plan, and take action. If you've taken the time to do the work by the time you get to this point, a lot has probably changed for you. I started to see the changes take shape in my life after three months. You never know how long something will take once you get started. If you haven't started, go back and find the exercises that you are ready for and get moving!

You learned what habits you want to change and decided that you don't want to stay in the same place that you have been. You've learned that bitching and complaining does nothing in your life but keep you stagnant. And surprisingly enough, you discovered a deeper part of yourself that you didn't know existed.

There are many stages of change that a person goes through in their life. Change is inevitable and it is always coming about in ways that we do not expect it. We lose our jobs. A close family member passes away. We move to a new state to start over. No matter what the change is, it is a new stage to be explored and handled with care.

We really touched on the plethora of ways that you can grow mentally, spiritually, emotionally, and physically. You stuck with it even when it was hard and now you are ready to go out into the world and share the new you. At first, it is going to feel foreign, and then you are going to realize that you love the skin that you are in. It will take time, but you got this. Your mind is more open to receiving what is out there so go and take a chance. I am so proud of you!

Loving yourself is not about getting rid of pieces of yourself because you hate them. It is about loving the you that you know and understanding who you are more fully. Every obstacle you come across will look small because you have built the mental fortitude to take care of anything that comes along your path. You will no longer stand down from the challenge. You will fight it head on and win! Sometimes, you will lose, but you will be ready to pick yourself back up and tell the world, "Hey World, you hit like a bitch!" Courtesy of Zendaya.

If I could put my transformative journey into a short synopsis, it would go something like this: Changing has opened my eyes to the ways that I move in this world. I feel happier, lighter, more successful and overall, I am a happy person because of the things that I changed. It was not an easy process, and it helped so much.

I read a long time ago that your attitude is everything and I have learned through this process that it is true. You may not be happy that you have to change some major, or minor, things about yourself. I am not telling you to change them for me, your mom or your kids. I am telling you that when you decide to change, you feel better about the life that you have before you. You can make a difference in your career, relationships, and yourself just by changing your perspective on what life has to offer.

You do not have to wallow in the ick any longer. Make the change! Understand that you are the master of the life . There will be situations and challenges that you will have to face, and this book is a beacon of hope for those who believe that it can be done. You may not be ready to be alone, or to make the changes, and that is ok. I want you to know that the world that you live in right now is the same one that has you where you are today. So, what are you waiting for?

Resistance is the thief of your future. The more you resist the path that you are on in life, the further away you get from your goals. You may not know what that resistance looks like yet, because you have not pushed yourself to change as much as you have in these moments. I know that you are ready. Pick the area of change that you would like to pursue, whether it is mentally, emotionally, or physically, and start there. Push through your resistance and watch your whole world blossom before your eyes.

I don't expect you to change overnight and neither should you. We should set some real expectations here. You may have already started your journey, or this book may have been your first step to making the changes that you want, so be patient with yourself. Some days you will get up and not want to work on yourself. Some days you will go gung-ho in the transformative space. It is your right to do whatever you want.

Where do you go from here? Well, you have two options.

Number one. Do nothing. That's right, put this book down, give it away and literally do nothing with the rest of your life. Change is hard, I get it. But what is harder? Looking at your life right now, knowing that you could have changed it and instead you decided to stay there until you fell into the same hole you did to pick up this book in the first place. If that is what you want to do, I wish you the best of luck.

Number two. If you haven't started already, go back through this book and start making some changes. See this book as a jumpstart to your journey. Understand that you do not have to do everything in this book all at once. Pick one place and start there. Healing is not a linear path. Sometimes you will start at point A and go to point C, then to point G. All you have to know is that your journey starts with one choice. Your body, mind and soul know exactly what you need to do. All you have to do is listen to them.

Here's the thing, I am not here to tell you what you have to change or that you should change. I want you to discover who you are so that you show up more confident in the world. Sometimes we need a push in the right direction without someone telling us where to go and how to do things. You get the choice of what you want to change. You get to choose the life that you want to be a part of. You get to choose who you want to be. I am here to guide you through that journey, not live it for you. You may not know right this instant what you want to change, or maybe you have been thinking about it up to this point. Either way, that change will have an impact on everything that you do in life from now on.

Be mindful that this journey is a marathon, not a sprint. It took me three months to see changes from my initial no alcohol challenge. Yours may be more time or it may be less. The thing to remember is that comparison is the thief of joy. There are billions of people on this planet, and everyone will have their own journey to happiness. No one's life looks the same. It is all a process. You never know what is going to happen, but if you are ready to start the next chapter, start slowly.

I leave you with this. While on a date with my boyfriend, I realized that I honestly didn't like who I was before I decided to stop drinking. I was angry. I was mean. I was an outright bitch. I was constantly in a place where

I didn't feel true to myself, and I felt as if I was doing things to fit in with the people I associated with.

Then, I found myself.

That was the key that I had been missing, and my goal is to help you find the key to your existence. You didn't pick up this book just to see what some random millennial did to change their life. You resonated with the title, the inside flap, the testimonials, or the back of this book. It prompted you to make a change. So, let's go!

Let's make some changes and see where we are in a year.

Afterword

As the year ends, I have been listening to and reading personal development books. I know that there are things in my life that I still want to accomplish. I want to make sure that I grow steadily and that my foundation is strong. I decided to let go of the outcome, which over the years has really been hard for me. I participated in many coaching programs that I may not have taken seriously when I first started. I have books that I read that I didn't act on, completely.

As I read *Many Lives, Many Masters* by Brian L Weiss, M.D., I realized that the one thing that controlled me was fear. As I listened to *No Excuses* by Brian Tracy, he said that "Fear paralyzes action". That is what we as people have been doing for years. We either let fear paralyze us or we let it control our reaction to the things that are happening in life.

In *Many Lives, Many Masters*, the Master Spirit said to Dr. Weiss through Catherine, *"You are correct in assuming this is the proper treatment for those in the physical state. You must eradicate the fears from their minds. It is a waste of energy when fear is present. It stifles them from fulfilling what they were sent here to fulfill. Take your cues from your surroundings. They must first be put into a level very, very deep… where they no longer can feel their body. Then you can reach them. It's only on the surface… that the troubles lie. Deep within their soul, where the ideas are created, that is where you must reach them.*

"Energy… everything is energy. So much is wasted. The mountains… inside the mountain it is quiet; it is calm at the center. But on the outside is where the trouble lies. Humans only see the outside, but you can go much deeper. You have to see the volcano. To do it you have to go deep inside.

"To be in physical state is abnormal. When you are in spiritual state, that is natural to you. When we are sent back, it's like being sent back to something we do not know. It will take us longer. In the spirit world you have to wait, and then you are renewed. There is a state of renewal. It's a dimension like the other dimensions, and you have almost succeeded in reaching that state…"

I am writing these final thoughts on January 1, 2024. I am waiting for my breakfast, and I look back at 2023 and all of the accomplishments that I have achieved, and I am so very proud of myself. Yesterday I woke up to a text from a friend of mine that said "Congrats on your 1-year journey. I am so proud of you." My eyes were tearing up because not only was it a sweet message, but it also let me know that people were watching me. People see the changes that I am actively making in my life and are taking notice. That feels so good and it was never for them. It was for me.

I learned that the one person I was neglecting and not showing respect to was myself. I have been in situations that I got myself into and at no point did I check myself to make sure that I was not being disrespected in any way. Some things came to light yesterday and I realize that I need to better protect myself and my energy from those who try to destroy or diminish it.

I woke up this morning and wrote in my journal. I finally chose my focus word for the year and where I am going.

At my last NET session on the 28th, I talked to Lindsey about life and things that were taking place. One of the things that we worked on and released was loving myself and being able to cycle through the love that I am willing to show myself. There is so much that I want to give and that I give to others because love is great and being kind takes nothing. In that same breath, I have been giving and giving to others without getting that back and oftentimes I do not have any left for myself.

This year's focus word, 2024, is self-fulfillment.

My journal has a few lists in it that I want to complete and one of them is how I will show myself love, my energy leaks and where I want things to change in my life. In these upcoming months I want to show myself the love, care and respect that I have been giving to others all this time. My first step is acknowledging what I want and finding a way to get it. I want to be a bit more connected to myself and my body than I have been and thought about starting yoga again. I hung out with a friend of mine, and she told me about a workshop called Flows and Grows. It is a three-day workshop geared towards aligning yourself and your goals.

I was thinking about how I was going to afford it, and not in the sense of I didn't have the money. It was more in the sense of am I going to use my emergency fund money to fund it. Ironically, I had money in savings to be used on myself that I had not touched yet. There was more than enough money for this workshop, with some left over. I signed up for the workshop. Now, one of the best parts about signing up for this workshop was that if you signed up before January 1st, you got an unlimited Flows package that allowed you to take as many yoga classes as you want the whole month. Talk about alignment.

I am very excited about what this new year is going to be, and I am so glad that I got to share it with you. By the time this book reaches you, we may be past 2024 altogether.

Thank you for picking up this book and learning about yourself. It was an amazing journey, and I hope the very same for you.

If you have read through this book and your life has been changed from it, please email me and share your stories at <u>desirablephoenix@gmail.com</u>. If you are interested in working with me further, please find me on Instagram and Tik Tok @phoenixofchange.